A THEATRICAL TRIP
FOR A WAGER

HORTON RHYS
[Morton Price]

A THEATRICAL TRIP

FOR A WAGER

First Published London, 1861
Reissued 1969 by
BENJAMIN BLOM, INC.
New York

First Published 1861
Reissued 1969 by
Benjamin Blom, Inc., Bronx, New York 10452

Library of Congress Catalog Card Number 73-81217

Printed in U.S.A. by
NOBLE OFFSET PRINTERS, INC.
NEW YORK 3, N. Y.

A Theatrical Trip

FOR

A WAGER!

THROUGH

CANADA AND THE UNITED STATES.

BY

CAPTAIN HORTON RHYS,

("MORTON PRICE.")

Author of "Tit for Tat," "Folly," "All's Fair in Love and War," &c. &c.

LONDON:

PUBLISHED FOR THE AUTHOR BY

CHARLES DUDLEY, 4, AGAR STREET, WEST STRAND.

1861.

THIS

UNPRETENDING, AND (I TRUST) UNOFFENDING LITTLE VOLUME, IS

Dedicated

(BY PERMISSION),

TO

HIS GRACE

HENRY CHARLES, DUKE OF BEAUFORT,

BY HIS OLD SCHOOLFELLOW,

CHARLES HORTON RHYS,

("MORTON PRICE.")

Chadderton Hall, Lancashire,
November 1st, 1861.

ADDRESS.

Friends, R——eaders, and Countrymen, until just as I was *about* sending this my Bantling to be brought out, or, in other words, this my Book to be printed, it never occurred to me that the same *should* have a Dedication. I turned me round in thought, and mentally reviewed the names of those to whom I might apply without fear of refusal, or worse—suspicious or supercilious inquiries into the character of the production to which they were solicited to stand sponsor. While thus calculating and " concluding," kind Fate conducted me into the presence of an old friend and schoolfellow (may I here throw up my hat, and cry " Floreat Etona?") whom I had not seen for many years, but of whom I had a keen recollection as a good schoolfellow, a first-rate sportsman, and princely patron of all things *deserving* of patronage. Ere the warm pressure of his hand had left my palm, and the kindly tone of his voice had ceased to echo in my ear, I *felt* " I should have asked him"   *   *   *   *

I *did,* and the result was, the preceding page.

A Theatrical Trip for a Wager!

CHAPTER I.

WRITE a Book! Well, why shouldn't I?—many a more stupid fellow than I, have "gone and done it," ere this. Let me see!—educated at Eton, many years in the army at home and abroad, a wanderer in many lands, with a smattering of every language under the sun;—write a Book! I rather think so—and here goes!

Now I beg, at starting, emphatically to state that if anybody takes offence at anything I write, I don't care, because it is all true—not founded on facts, but facts *in puribus;* and I would, also, in order to avoid the charge of obtaining readers under false pretences, beg to inform all those who being led to suppose, by the title of my book (my book!) that they will gain information as to the time it takes, or the distance you have to travel to get from one place to another, &c., &c., &c., that they will spend their money quite uselessly in purchasing it.

This being my maiden effort, I am ignorant whether the Printer or Publisher corrects all inaccuracies of Spelling, Grammar, and so forth, or not; I can only hope he does, for I write as I think—first come, first served, truth uppermost, and shame the D——l, (not the Printer's of that ilk, but the other.) My peregrinations and experiences will go down as I remember them, and at just about the pace that a school-boy commits to paper some few hundred lines of Virgil given him by his Pedagogue as an *"imposition,"* so, my dear readers, *(my dear readers!")* excuse mistakes, if you please.

On a very wet February English evening, or rather night, or I should say morning, for it was after midnight, "there might have been seen" a jovial party of some eighteen or twenty persons, all of the gender male, sitting round—that is, up on one side and down the other of a long table in a large room, in a middling-sized Hotel in the greatest Garden in the world—to wit, Covent Garden, in the well-known City, or adjoining thereto, of London. (Writing this in America, I am obliged to particularize, as there is *a* London somewhere in Canada, which is, *or was,* you know, part of America; but it is *not* so large as our London, though that may not be generally known *here.* Indeed, I am sure. But I am getting away from the "thread of my narrative.") Well, this jovial party, that is, a party assembled for the purpose of jollity (jolly old word—all my smattering of language has never enabled me to find a true translation, or equivalent; the French try it, but it isn't a bit like it), are so assembled, and it would seem, have been so assembled for some time, as sundry empty Champagne bottles and the wretched remains of two swingeing bowls of Punch attest. The conversation is animated, the subjects thereof entirely Dramatic, Operatic, and thoroughly Theatrical.

This Supper Party is conclusive of an Amateur Performance which has this night taken place at the * * * * Theatre, half at least of the jolly ones being aiders and abettors therein; the others invited friends, also theatrically disposed as far as the *wings* are concerned, but as yet unknown to the footlights, save and excepting one or two, who having occasionally exhibited themselves at *Trotterbury* and *Weathertown,* think themselves somebodies, but are scarcely recognised as *bonâ fide* Amateurs—strong suspicions being extant that these said exhibitions contribute as much to the exhibitors pockets as to their pastime.

At the head of the table is seated the chairman of this convivial gathering. He has just resumed his seat amid considerable applause, and "one cheer more" having concluded his "thanks for the honour they have done him in drinking his health," and, indeed, he has made quite a long speech for an Amateur. There, however, seems to have been matter in this said speech, at which one or more of those assembled, demur, for shortly after our story opens, and before the small hours had obtained much size, a conversation ensued which I will presently chronicle.

Viewing the whole proceedings with a somewhat cynical eye, and looking upon the "upstanding" portion as a decided bore, was a round-faced, round-bodied, hairy-looking individual, seated midway down the table ; and next to him, on his right, reposed (for he appeared to be asleep—an occasional puff of smoke issuing from his lips, alone deciding him to be animate), a very long man, lank in hair and limp in body—the latter, at the time we narrate, forming the half of an O, and his legs two-thirds of a triangle. We will call these individuals Smith and Brown.

SMITH (loq.) "So you really think, R——, that it is possible for an Amateur to be as good as a Professional ?"

R., "Undoubtedly. I, of course, mean a *gentleman* Amateur. Some of our best actors were amateurs, and were as good then as they are now. Toole, of the Adelphi, for instance."

S., (superciliously) "Ah, a low-comedy man."

R., "Exactly."

S., "I am speaking of the line of business you prefer."

R., "Which is that ?"

S., "Light comedy, Charley Mathews, eh ?" (nudging the limp man.)

BROWN (slightly starting) "Eh ?—yes, good !"

R., "Oh, light comedy. Well, what have you to say about light comedy ?"

S., "Simply, that no man that isn't bred up to the profession——"

FACETIOUS LISTENER (interrupting) "Sire, actor—dam, actress."

S., "I didn't say that."

SAME PARTY. "No one said you did." (slight laughter unpleasant to SMITH.)

S., "I say that no man that hasn't studied the Profession with a view to adopting it from his youth can ever be a finished, or even tolerable light comedian—a *Charles Surface*, a *Rover*, a *Don Cæsar*, a *Sir Charles Coldstream*, a (*pointedly*,) R., had played the character that evening) *Citizen Sangfroid*——"

R., "Oh!"

S., "It's all very well to say 'Oh!'"

SECOND FACETIOUS INDIVIDUAL. "Not always," (bestowing a pinch upon the drowsy BROWN, whose exclamation thereupon, immediately corroborated S. F. I's. assertion.)

S., "Now, look here, R——. (R., did so.) You think yourself no end of an Amateur, don't you?"

R., "My dear sir, modesty forbids——"

S., "Oh, bosh! You are modest with a vengeance, to play *Delicate Ground* to a London audience, just after Anderson has been doing it!"

R., "Well——"

FACETIOUS MAN. "Anderson, or self?"

R., (confidently) "Both."

INCORRIGIBLE WRETCH. "Good!"

S., (resuming) "You wouldn't like your talent to be tested by an audience that didn't know you were as the bills call you, or I should say, as you call yourself in the bills, 'The celebrated Amateur, Captain H. R——,' and with a company of Professionals——"

R., "I have already done so."

S., "Once——"

R., "Once. But you are monopolizing all the conversation. Do bring your catechism to an end, and let us know the drift of it."

S., "I should like to know whether you, a crack Amateur, as I suppose you consider yourself, seriously think that you could make money by acting, where you would not be recognised and receive the leniency usually shown to an Amateur."

R., "Seriously, I feel sure I could."

S., "Bravo! That song you sang was your own composition, wasn't it?"

R., " Did you ever hear it before ?"

S., " No, and don't care if I never hear it again."

R., " Ah, somebody told me the other day ' 'twas a pity Smith ever attempted to sing,' "

S., " Indeed. Do you think you would have been encored in it, if you had been a Professional, and the song written by some one else ?"

R., " Of course, I do."

S., " Ha, ha ! Why, my dear sir, you wouldn't, couldn't, as a singer and actor, make five pounds in a fortnight."

R., " I would make five hundred in a year !"

S., " I'll bet you five hundred you don't !"

R., (excited) " Done ! There's a fiver (producing a piece of paper representing that amount) to sign articles to-morrow morning !"

S., " Agreed. Where are you ?" (pocketing the note.)

R., " Your sleepy friend there, knows. Come with him, I fancy he will go you halves. Two o'clock, Lunch, and an amicable arrangement of our argument—to the tune of a *monkey*."*

This being acceded to by Smith, and meeting with an approving grunt from his particular friend, Brown, thus ended the " commencement du fin" of my wager—in the bold attempt to win which all that is, in this to-be-celebrated book narrated, occurred.

This little matter settled, and Messrs. Smith and Brown silenced for awhile, the remainder of the *evening* passed merrily enough ; and having only thus recorded the Party, that all whom it may concern shall know the origin of my having cause for thus " rushing into print," I will dismiss it forthwith, and proceed to place before my readers a verbatim copy of a document to which I, in conjunction with Messrs. Smith and Brown, appended our autographs before three o'clock of the afternoon of the day following that of the Party.

February 12th, 1859.

We, the undersigned A. SMITH and B. BROWN, conjointly bet CAPTAIN H. R., the sum of five hundred pounds that he does not, in any country other than Great Britain or Ireland, by his talents as an

---

* " Tattersall" slang, meaning £500.

actor, author, singer, or composer, separately or collectively, clear the sum of five hundred pounds over and above all expenses other than those of Board and Lodging and personal expenditure. We, the undersigned, further agree that CAPTAIN H. R., shall be permitted to take with him and employ, as assistant, any actress he may choose, provided she has not up to this present date appeared as an actress in London, Liverpool, or Manchester, and has not played an engagement as leading lady in any Theatre whatever; and it is further stipulated that any engagement she may play *singly* shall not be included in the terms of this wager. Twelve calendar months from the date of his (CAPTAIN H. R.'s) first appearance in such country as he may select, to be the time allotted for the completion of his task, and the bet to be won or lost in eighteen calendar months from the date of this agreement. We hereby make a deposit of fifty pounds (CAPTAIN H. R., doing the same), and the whole of the money, One Thousand Pounds (£500 aside) to be made good on or before the Eighteenth day of March next, when, to prevent the possibility of after-dispute, CAPTAIN H. R., is to name the lady whom he has engaged to accompany him and determine the day of his departure. It is further stipulated that CAPTAIN H. R., shall travel and make and play his engagements under an assumed and fictitious name, and shall not, previous to, or upon his arrival at each place as he may determine upon visiting, make his real name known; and shall abstain from calling on private friends or newspaper editors, and from signing his own name to any play, or pamphlet, or letter; and we, the undersigned, hereby agree to abide by the returns of expenditure and profits which shall be furnished to us from time to time by CAPTAIN H. R. The same being guaranteed to be true and correct upon word and honor, as an officer and a gentlemen. And to this we do now append our names.

A. SMITH.

B. BROWN.

I, the undersigned, hereby agree to all and each of the foregoing agreements and conditions.

H. R.

This interesting and novel Document being safely deposited in the hands of a gentleman, better known to Sporting than Theatrical circles, I bestirred me forthwith to carry out an idea which had occurred to me at the time of making the wager.

A short time previous, I had gone by invitation to assist in some Amateur Performances at Exeter and Plymouth, and there I had seen a young actress, whom I shall call Lucille, whose great beauty of voice, extreme youth, and lady-like deportment had much interested me. It flashed upon me when my opponents, Messrs. Smith and Brown, were comforting themselves in the thought that they had pretty well shut me out of all chance of obtaining any great female talent, that this was my chance, if I could persuade her to brave the perils of the deep, &c., &c. I may here state I had quite determined on making America and Canada the field of my operations. So off I wrote to Edinburgh, where I knew she was then playing at the Theatre Royal (since transmogrified, I hear, into a Post Office) third to the Misses St. George and Louise Keeley, got a satisfactory answer, and thereupon arranged for her to close her engagement and to meet me at Leamington, which she did shortly, accompanied by her mother. We then played with the A. B. C. Club (Amateurs), and I, of course, was only too delighted to see that Lucille, in her *début*, under my management, made before a most fastidious audience, a decided hit *as an actress*; she played the small but pretty part of *Mary*, in *Naval Engagements*. In her singing I had already full confidence, and my grand object was now to obtain for her a London appearance, and (I prayed) success.

This was speedily effected through Mr. M., the agent of the lessee of Drury Lane, who was in want of a *prima donna* to take the part of *Susan*, in Mr. Tully's new opera of *William and Susan* (pirated, of course, from the celebrated drama of that name), which, after one or two delays, was produced at the said theatre on the 28th of February, to a crowded house; and I am sure the veritable *Mons. Dufard*, in *The First Night*, never felt more excited for the success of his " child, Rose," than did I for the success of this young lady. Suffice it to say that she was encored in her first song (the only *solo* set down for her in the piece), and played and sang throughout well enough to elicit the praise of the London Press, *without exception.* The opera ran until the close of the season, and great was the surprise and demur of Messrs. Smith and Brown when, on the Eighteenth day of March, I notified to them that I had selected the *prima donna* of Drury Lane to accompany me across the Atlantic !

They had, however, no help for it, the bond ran thus : " provided she has not *up to this present date* appeared," &c., &c.

The twenty-third of April arrived, the Cunard steamer, " Niagara," (Capt. Millar), sailed from Liverpool, and amongst the passengers "might have been observed" a gentleman and two ladies busily engaged in watching their man servant making frantic efforts to fish out what was wanted, from what was not, of an apparently endless confusion of luggage, for safe consignment to the said ladies' and gentleman's cabins, or state rooms, as they are, in the *lucus-a-non-lucendo* style, termed.

I have just read a book, entitled " Weld's Vacation Tour through the United States and Canada," wherein is such an admirable description of a similar voyage, that to save myself the trouble of writing, and also the possible charge of piracy, I will refer my readers to Mr. Weld for all information of the incidents, accidents, amusements, and occupations concomitant to a passage across the Atlantic, and say no more of the trip than conduces to the safe conduct of my story.

Capitain.Horton.Rhys.del.

AN ICEBERG BY MOONLIGHT.

C. J. Culliford, lith. 22. Southampton. St. Strand.W.C.

CHAPTER II.

My pleasure was great on finding among the passengers a certain Captain B., who having got tired of soldiering at home, had effected an exchange from the 13th Light Infantry into the Canadian Rifles, and was on his way to join. This was a blessing—we were a "Party" forthwith, and as we were fortunate enough to have a beautiful passage, the said party managed to pass the ten days it took our good ship to accomplish the distance to Halifax, very *jollily*, (this word will often occur, as I like it.) We had occasional Concerts in the saloon, grave affairs, save when Captain B., in singing "The Cork Leg," and acting the same, a lurch of the vessel conducted him to a premature conclusion in the lap of some young lady, or when the Purser, who was a sort of nautical *Sam Cowell*, allowed his feelings to carry him away into *comicalities* which sent the men portion of his audience into a roar, and the ladies out of the saloon in confusion. Oh, my fellow voyagers, remember ye "My jolly ould sthick!" Wonderful games of *Whist*, in which I did not join, and "Shuffle-board," which I did ; then we had a never-failing source of amusement in the presence of a remarkably tall individual, who suffered us (whom he good-naturedly called *youngsters*, though I question if some of *us* were not quite as old, and older than himself), to play all sorts of games with.

We then called him "Long Tom," so shall I now, and should he see these pages, he will thereby know I bear him in pleasant memory.

Captain B's skirmishes with him were incessant, and the passengers would frequently form themselves into a sort of Box audience to witness the absurdities that passed between them. One day it was carried in council that "Long Tom" was far too good a fellow, and a great deal too large an object to go at large any longer, and that, for his own sake, it were advisable that he should be placed under surveillance. Consequently it was determined that he should be sold to the highest bidder at Public Auction, and sold he was, after some spirited competition amongst the ladies, being knocked down to Lucille for——, I forget the price; since which time she has always called him *her property*, but like most properties not settled on oneself, he, of course, " passed away" at the conclusion of the voyage, and I have not seen our long friend since.

He was one of those rare good fellows that time and absence make you the more wishful to meet again.

We had but two rough days, and ere they arrived every one had found their sea-legs, and the Steward did not reap much benefit by absentees at feeding time. I may here remark that on board the Cunard vessels, of which the " Niagara" was one, *the fare you get is well worth the fare you give;* a better table I never saw.

Well, on the evening of our tenth day we touched at Halifax, and for the first time looked down upon the land of America* (or rather the lamps thereof, for it was too dark to discern more than a dim outline of the shore); Halifax, as all know, or all ought to know, is under the sovereignty of our Gracious Queen, and ruled by her by proxy.

As soon as the vessel was alongside the Wharf, among other be- siegers were a posse of "*sojer*" officers, who clamoured and clattered until they had found the object of their search—viz., a lady who had been my positive aversion during the voyage. The airs she gave herself were immense ; a sort of Aidé-camp always attended her in the shape of a young man who spoke incessantly with the least pleasant of Irish brogues (the Dublin accent) of his " toitled acqueentance," and paid immense attention to the fine lady's daughter ! The *party* proved to be the wife,—I beg her pardon, *Lady* I should have said, and daughter of some military Big-wig somewhere in those diggings, and the Irish- man was something between a soldier and a civilian, not quite either, going to the same place, in the commissariat or something. I predict *his* attentions have been long ere this dispensed with, for, unless I am mistaken more than is my wont, one of the before-mentioned officers

---

* Nova Scotia strictly speaking, but invariably hailed by the stranger as the first port and key of the New World.

had somewhere seen, some time before, the young lady ; at all events he took great care of her, and poor " Pill-Garlick" looked on from amid a pile of wraps, &c., with a most dejected countenance.

I was quite astonished at the amount of *swagger* possessed and shown by these gentlemen—I mention it not that the said swagger did *me* any harm, or because any of them trod on *my* toes, without begging my "*pawdon*," but, that any young officer (of course an old one is incorrigible) who may chance to read this book, may know an old one's opinion on military swagger. *It is the worst swagger of all !*—that of brief authority, that of wealth, title, beauty—(oh yes, beauty swaggers too, be it in woman or man ; proud beauty, impudent beauty, swaggers equally in its own fashion),—these are bad enough, but the swagger of a man in a red coat is unendurable ; it approaches nearer to the insolence of Flunkeyism than anything else.

There were a good many Americans on board, and their remarks upon the "*offishness*" of some of these embryo warriors were smart enough ; Americans form their opinions, in a great measure, of English soldiers from those they see at Halifax. In the Canadas they are so much scattered, and, by the constant stream of American visitors, so much Americanized, that they are hardly looked upon by the latter as types of English soldiery. Nor are they ; for if an officer in Canada gave himself the absurd airs, i.e. *swagger,* that many, indeed, most of most of them do, in her Majesty's colonies, he would be sent to Coventry by both Americans and Canadians.

I shall not beg pardon for this digression, as is the Novelist's wont, for, as I said before, I shall say what I like, and, therefore, without further parley take up my story from the time of my fellow passengers departure under safe, that is, military escort.

On inquiry, we found that our ship would rest from her labours for a very short time, and that any one desirous of stretching their legs on shore had better be sharp about it. Naturally, as an every-day matter, I am one of the coolest and most self-collected of human beings (friend *David,* I turn to thee for confirmation of the same !) How happened it, then, that for many hours before the vessel reached the Wharf, and as she steamed past the long line of lights reflected in the darkness of the night, on, down, and through the murky waters, like Phosphoric flashes—how was it that this self-collected gentleman might have been, and *was* noticed to be suffering under considerable nervous excitement ? Not the joyous excitement visible in the faces of many who were then gazing for the first time on as much as they could see of a fresh land, nor yet the excitement of some, consequent on unfounded suspicion that the Boston baggage might by some jugglery be sent on shore at Halifax ; not either the excitement of meeting friends, for *I* had none to meet, but——I must digress again.

Know ye then, oh my readers, that from youth upwards I had been superstitious—my family have ever been so. I would see a ladder " *somewhere first*" before I would go underneath it ; looking at the new moon through glass was bad luck for a month ; not taking off my hat to a Magpie, when going hunting, (*myself* not the Magpie) was provocative of a blank day, or prognostic of a broken collar-bone, *cum multis aliis* of such like. In Mesmerism I had, reasonably, a moderate confidence, but up to a month previous to my leaving England I had a profound contempt for all believers in *spirit-rapping*, and about that time communicated the same to a friend of mine who happened to be dining with me at the Regent Hotel, Leamington.

" Well," said my friend (whom I will call *Jones*) " I am rather glad to hear you say so," (referring to my expressed disbelief;) " for though you laugh at *spirit-rapping*, you seem to believe in the active agency of spirits over our thoughts and deeds."

R., " For good or evil, yes."

J., " Please explain, before I tell you something about *spirit-rapping*, how you think spirits influence thought and deed ?"

R., " Simply thus : One spirit sayeth ' It is very nice ;' the other, ' It is very *wrong*'—the flesh listeneth and answereth ' It is delightful.' The *knowledge* replieth ' It is wicked ;'—the worldly man *he* tosseth up, and chance directs *his* action ; the righteous man *instanter* sides with the better spirit, and the twain tumble back the *worse* to his master, the D——l, for fresh instructions."

J., " What an extraordinary idea !"

R., " It is mine, and now for yours."

J., " You have seen my eldest boy ; he is a *medium*."

R., " A how much !"

J., " A vehicle for conveying messages between the mortal and immortal."

R., " A sort of *male* coach, eh ?"

J., " Good ; but I want to be serious. This child has told me extraordinary things ; he is very delicate, and his mother objects strongly to his being employed as a *spirit-questioner*."

R., " Sensible woman !" (sotto voce, I saw Jones was in earnest.)

J., " But if you would like to have your eyes opened and your disbelief a little shaken, come home with me, and I will get him to try."

R., " Done with you, let us——"

J., " One moment; I must tell you through this child some months ago, I was told of the death of a near and dear relative in Pennsylvania."

R., " That must have been the Spirit of the Atlantic Cable !"

J., " Come along, you must judge for yourself——"

In half-an-hour I was in Jones' house, and watching, with a great deal more interest than I expected, the performance of the child, who, seated in front of a closed cottage piano with his small hands rested thereon, was seriously engaged asking the following question :—" Are there any spirits in the room ?"

My whispered reply, " Whisky," was almost sternly reproved by Jones, who seemed to have his life depending on the expected answer, which I was assured would come in the shape of a knock if any there were, and sure enough come it did, loud, clear, and imperative.

" Who the dickens did that ?" I said, certainly startled.

" Hush !"

" How many spirits are present ?" whined the small boy, wherupon came a succession of knocks, raps, scratches and creakings, out of which Jones counted *fifty* or *sixty*, and in amazement I looked round the little room, and thought of *crinoline*.

" Well, I never !" I said ; " how *do* you do that ?"

" Hush !" said the parent.

The medium then asked numerous questions, all of which were replied to by numerous sounds of discomfort from the bewitched Cottage, into which I looked, and over and under, behind, and all round; but nothing could I discover; I saw the grave face of the mother and father (the latter's had assumed a preternatural sombreness), and gradually, but irresistibly, I became engrossed in the proceedings. Turning to me, Jones loquitur in a whisper, which quite made me jump, " Would *you* like to ask anything of the spirits ?"

" Oh, yes," I answered, plucking up, " Fire away ! Am I going a journey ?"

Answer—" Yes."

" Where ?"

Answer—" America."

" Good !" (didn't know that the Jones family knew *that*.) " What am I going to do there ?"

No answer.

" Is any one going with me ?"

Answer—" Yes."

" How many ?"

Answer—" Three." (*that* the Jones family could *not* have known.)

" Shall I succeed in my enterprise ?"

No answer.

" Ah," said Jones, " they wish to dissuade you from going."

" Shall I arrive safely in America ?"

No answer.

" Better not ask," suggested Jones.

" Oh, hang it!" I said, quite excited, " let us ask again."

At last, after putting the question four or five times, there came a most decided *double* knock, which being interpreted, meant " No !"

I sought to know what was to happen; whether I was to be burnt, blown up, drowned, or digested by cannibals, but deuce another reply could be obtained ; and considerably puzzled, I returned home, and if I didn't dream of ships on fire and signal guns, and roaring waters, it's a pity.

Those who superficially know me, will scarcely credit me when I say that, from that time until that at which I so summarily broke off the *thread of my narrative* to recount this spirit-rapping business, the recollection of that child, and the haunted cottage, and the supernatural sounds therein, out, or on (as they might have been) were never absent from my mind—I couldn't bear the word, "shipwreck," to meet my eyes in the newspaper, and Lucille nearly killed me one day by asking "If there were any life-preservers on board?" However, my reader is now gratified (of course) by knowing that the ship has reached the shores of America without mishap, and can enter into my feelings of impatience to set foot on *terra firma*, and thereby, as I thought, break the spell which was on me, and give the lie to the Spirits of the Piano.

I had never mentioned a syllable of this spirit-rapping prophecy to Lucille, or to her mother, and when I declared my intention to the former of going on shore the moment the ship was alongside, the expression of my face was such as to cause her to say, "Are you ill? Let me go with you."

"But you are not *ready*," I said, impatiently.

"Oh," she answered, "five minutes will do that."

"Yes," I whispered, "but five minutes may *do* me;" and in five seconds I was at the gangway, over the plank, and on American soil. Not content with walking on the Wharf, I took a spin up the gravel road about fifty yards and back, and came on board again a perfect firework of spirits (*not* rapping ones;) I insisted on Lucille's coming on shore, which she did, and we wandered about the most sombre looking town I ever saw, until the red, blue, and white stars of an exploding rocket, high up in "Heaven's blue vault," enlightened us as to the necessity of retracing our steps and getting on board.

On board we got with the last of the coal, and to bed we went quite "jolly," which jollity, however, was somewhat disturbed on the following day by the Captain saying in reply to some remark of mine about Halifax, "Halifax. Oh, we don't call Halifax, America!" *My* spirits sank instanter to Zero, and the *others* were in the ascendant; however, our voyage across the Bay of Fundy was so tranquil (it can be rough when it chooses) my mind was comparatively easy, and I listened to the conversation of the newly-arrived American portion of the passengers with tranquillity and amusement.

*   *   *   *   *   *

" A smart man, sir !—a darn'd smart——I beg your pardon." This was the exclamation of a gentleman, who, as I entered the saloon, rather late for breakfast, having finished his own, was coming out, and walking one way and talking another, trod somewhat heavily on my slippered feet.

" Don't mention it, sir, 'twas my fault more than your's," I politely replied (fortunately my toes hadn't to make the reply instead of my tongue.)

" Now, I guess that's a Britisher, he's so darn'd polite," said he audibly. The Steward told me afterwards that he, the Yankee, for of course such he was, came direct to him and asked my name, occupation, destination, &c., &c. ; and when told I was a Captain, at once ejected me from his further consideration, together with a demonstration from his mouth, of which abomination more anon.

I had my breakfast, and then proceeded to the deck to enjoy a pipe ; in the process of which, I suddenly found myself nudged in the side by my heavy-treading acquaintance of an hour previous.

" First journey here, stranger ?"

" Yes," I said ; " it is."

" Going to Canada, I guess ?"

" No, not at present."

These four words appeared quite to surprise him, and " Wa-al," he said, " if that Steward ain't the blessedest——I understood him to say as you were a Captain."

" So I am."

" Then what the——'scuse me ; what on airth are you come here for ?"

" To America?" I answered innocently, " to see the country, to study the people, and all the rest of it."

" Then I guess you'll go back again pretty considerable sleepy "

" Why so," said I curiously.

" Why ? Cause you'll have to keep your eyes so tarnation wide open to make that 'ere study of yourn worth the studyin', that it's darn'd little sleep you'll get here, that's a fact."

I laughed.

" Writin' a book," said he, interrogatively.

" May be,'" said I, comically.

" Darn'd if I did'nt think so !" said he, energetically ; and after a pause, he added thoughtfully, " A great country, a smart people."

Catching at the word " smart," I said, " You were saying some one was very *smart*, as we met at the saloon door. May I ask if it was any public man you alluded to ?"

He looked at me, put his finger to the side of his nose, and said, *à la* Clarke (the Strand Clarke), " You're beginning, you air."

I made a gesture of entire innocence of such a crime.

" Wa-al," he resumed, " I don't mind telling yew ; it will do for your book, ha, ha !"

" Well, if it is good enough, it may," I said, quietly.

He stared again, and then looking at me, he said, " I guess you'll hear more stories in America than you ever heard in the Old Country."

" *Greater ones*, I have no doubt," I answered, assentively.

A long and concentrated gaze, in which nothing escaped from my head to my feet, ended in his admiringly exclaiming, " I'm darn'd if they'll get much out of yew, any way they fix it, that's a fact."

I laughed a reply, and asked him, " if he would not tell me of the smart man I had alluded to ?"

" I had concluded not to tell yew, he answered ; " but I spose if I don't you'll put me down in that 'ere book of yourn as a—a—a bad specimen of a Yankee ?"

To this point-blank question I was obliged to make some answer, so said, " Very possibly," and offered him a cigar, which accepting, he told me the following *smart* story :—

" Up in our city there's a Quaker, tremenjous rich he is, too—part owner, and whole owner of a sight of ships—goes to all parts they do, and of course he insures them—that is, generally. Wa-al, this Fall, one of these ships—a reg'lar little fortune—she becomes over-due, she does—that is, there's nothing heerd on her, so Quaker becomes nervous, and wants to complete her insurance, which owing to some neglect at the Office, hadn't been done, and he calls pretty near every day. Wa-al, one day quite airly he comes, and says he to the Clerk, 'Friend,' says he, 'thou needst not trouble about the insurance, for I've heerd on the ship.' Clerk was d'rectly all business, he was, and for settling matters right away—the crittur wanted to get the Premium, he did, so, says he, 'Oh, it's all right!' and hands over the Policy papers; and Quaker puts 'em in his pocket without so so much as a thank'ee. Quaker *had* 'heerd on the ship.' *She had gone down, she had, and not a cent saved.* Smart man, that Quaker!"

The afternoon of the 6th of May saw us safe in Boston Harbour, and an hour or two after, we were comfortably housed in the "Parker House," a hostelrie, in that city, and I no longer hesitated to pronounce *the spirits* humbugs.

The Hotels here are called *Houses;* there's the "Revere House," "Fremont House," and "Parker's House"—the latter being mostly frequented by travellers and bachelors—and here a word of advice to all who may follow in my wake, which applies to every Hotel or *House* in every city and town throughout America and Canada. Be you travelling *en garçon,* or *en famille,* on your arrival at an Hotel, walk straight to the *Office,* state the strength of your party, the probable length of your stay, and your requirements, and *make the best bargain* you can. You will then get board and lodging as reasonably as in any country in the world; neglect to do this, and when you peruse your bill at the end of a week, or whenever it may be, if your eyes don't expand beyond their accustomed limits, I am no true historian. They don't *add* up your score, but *pile* it, and if you remonstrate, they coolly tell you it is their usual charge "*when no arrangement is made,*" which means they would have done it for half, sooner than you should have applied at another *House.*

Well, we are in Boston, Massachusetts, and "What do you think of it?" having been asked of me some dozen times within a few hours after my arrival, I will here chronicle what I *did* think of it. I thought it a remarkably clean, healthy-looking town ; hottish, but cooled down by an abundance of trees, which grow out of the pavement in a remarkable manner. Dickens was tickled by the innumerable sign-boards into fancying each street a scene in a Pantomime—I never got quite so far into my imagination as that, but I certainly was much struck by the immensity of outside advertising. Little need, I should say, for news-paper puffing, when so much is spent in paint and plaster, that all who run may read.

The country round is very uninteresting, and though we drove for hours on the day succeeding our arrîval, I saw nothing worthy of note.

Of course Lucille was greatly amused by the blackness of the waiters, who at the Parker House are all niggers, as nothing of higher grade than an Irishman would consent to be a servant or " helps," as they are called, in America; bless you, as " Britons never will be slaves," so *Yankees never will be servants.*   The chamber-maids are delicious ; they dress, and talk, and——well, here is a specimen, and as it was our first experience of the race, judge, oh, reader, for yourself, of our satisfaction— Lucille on going to her room in the course of our first evening, rang for some one to light the gas, and after some half-dozen applications to the bell-pull was honored with the presence of a female. I happened to enter the room at the same time, as the young lady's delay was annoying to my appetite, and the following strange colloquy ensued :—

" Please, light the gas for me."

" Guess I'm not your chamber-gal."

I must here tell you that this female, who wasn't a *chamber-gal,* was dressed in the height of the fashion. She had on a hoop which stood out under a pink gingham skirt, large and stiff as a gig umbrella—the effect of which was slightly marred by the same exposing to my delighted yet astonished eyes, as I followed her up the stairs, a pair of legs, the same size all the way up, encased in shocking dirty stockings, with shoes or slippers down at heel, in each of which was a good sized rat-hole ; her arms were naked to the shoulder, and decorated with a showy bracelet apiece; her neck was bare to——anywhere, and her hair frizzed out like a bunch of garden Endives.

Hearing her saucy reply, and feeling rather "*riled*" thereat, I roared in her ear, "What the devil are you, then?"

With a look of supreme contempt, she answered, as she *seated herself in a chair,* "I'm housekeeper, I am!"

To which Lucille said, "Then will you be kind enough to send some one to me?"

"Yon's the bell. Guess you're near'st it; but I don't mind if I do it, this time."

Lights up, and down she sat again. Eyeing Lucille, she said, "Guess you ain't got no hoop?"

"Oh, yes I have."

"Don't stick out much, I reckon! Mine does—fine!" (getting up, and turning round to exhibit her extent in that line.)

Concealing my inclination to scream, I said to Lucille, "That's something like a hoop. You must get one."

"That's so; guess we Boston gals knows a hoop when we sees one, and that sorter won't dew, any heow you can fix it!" and out she went.

Good lord! We looked at each other, and if we never laughed before, we did then.

CHAPTER III.

READER, hail ye from "ye City of Bladud?" Dost thou remember that city of Pumps and Palaces in the years previous to /45? Dost thou remember a little man; yea, a little and yet a great man? His hands were small, nearly as his gloves; his feet were small, almost as his boots; he was small in stature, and of fashionable form: that is, not *too* fat. In short, have you any recollection of "*Jacobus?*"—he was, in every sense of the word, a Bath beau. Was there a Ball, or Political Meeting, or, ye gods! an Amateur Performance, who knew so much of every requirement for the due carrying out of the same as *Jacobus?* Little thought I, when last I saw him with his little boots and little gloves, and little cane; and last, not least, his good dinner-loving face, walking down the handsomest shop street in the world (for its size)—viz., Milsom-street, Bath, that the next time I should shake him by the hand would be some fifteen years after, in the New World, even where my narrative, and the good ship, "Niagara," has now brought me—the City of Boston; such is the fact. Went to the Boston Theatre on the evening of our arrival, and the first person I saw in America, that I had ever seen before, was *Jacobus.* Of course, he did not recognise me; my assumed name assisting the disguise years had therewith clad me. He was little altered, save in size, which now had in breadth, compensated for what he lacked in length. *Jacobus'* form had filled out wonderfully; and his curly locks old Time had cooked in a way peculiarly his own; still there he was, hale and hearty as ever, and, when he found me out, appeared very glad to see me. Those of my readers who have recognised my sketch, will remember that its hero married previous to his going to America one of the cleverest, prettiest, and most lady-like of actresses. She is a prime favorite in the United States, and with pleasure I have lately learned that she is about to appear again in London.

After staying a short time at the Theatre, we saw Burton (since dead), " the greatest comic actor " in America, in his original part of *Toodles* (I thought Sir William Don superior in the same character, but did'nt get any one to agree with me but my own party.)   Went to the Howard Athenæum, a charming little theatre, and saw a Mr. Joseph P., and wife; the former as *Brutus*, in *Julius Cæsar*, and the latter as *Gertrude*, in *The Loan of a Lover*. It was a farewell benefit previous to " these talented artistes proceeding to England ;" and, as I believe, they *did* proceed and played somewhere in London, I shall say nothing of *our* opinion of their dramatic powers ; but I *must* give a sketch of one of the funniest scenes I ever witnessed in any theatre ; I have seen similar ones *since*, but novelty always makes impression, and my impression I now promulgate with a keen recollection of the amusement it then afforded me."

At the conclusion of the tragedy, Mr. P., was "*called.*" He appeared, and instead of retiring as the applause subsided, he put his feet between the two centre footlights, and commenced a speech ; in which, of course, regret at leaving his native country was scarcely counterbalanced by the " brilliancy of the offers he had received from numerous managers in England to cross the Atlantic, &c., &c."

Well, his speech was ended, and he was bowing himself off, when some attraction at the opposite wing caused Mr. P., to stay at his *exit* side, still bowing and glancing uneasily across the stage ; I must here mention that in the Pit, or what they call here the " Parquette," (Heaven knows where they got the word from) were some dozen or so of soldiers, at least they wore military uniforms, and several of these persons apparently excited, commenced a call for a Captain Somebody, whereupon, after a slight delay, there appeared at the R. first entrance a martial figure, corpulent withal, clad in the same costume as the gentlemen before mentioned in the Pit, who, without bow, or further preamble, marched up to the retiring P., (who seemed immensely relieved at his presence), and grasping him nervously by one hand, while the other seemed mysteriously confined behind him, commenced a speech, in which the public and private virtue of the said Mr. P., were prominently depicted. The great actor looked, *of course,* very much surprised, and when, suddenly, the corpulent Captain spasmodically withdrew his hand from under his coat tails, and produced a—well, I think it was a Pitcher—he was immensely affected. This Pitcher was supposed to be a present from his numerous admirers in Boston, " as a slight testimonial, &c., &c." At this juncture, the outward boundary of a lady's crinoline suddenly appeared at the L. first entrance ; but having mistaken its cue, as suddenly disappeared. Mr. Captain then proceeded to inquire for Mrs. P., of whose whereabouts Mr. P. protested, amid much laughter, his ignorance ; however, almost immediately, stepping to the left wing, and from thence handing in the crinoline proprietress, to whom the gallant Burgher presented a bracelet, which she gracefully kissed, ballet-bouquet fashion ; then Mr. P., returned thanks, commencing as follows :—" Ladies and Gentlemen, and Captain Somebody, surprise and astonishment at these *unexpected* and magnificent presents, which our 'umble efforts neither required nor deserved, &c., &c." Well, the house laughed, and so did we ; and laughing still, I will finish my first day at Boston.

I forgot to say in the foregoing, that I was in the course of the evening introduced to Mr. Barry, the lessee of the Boston Theatre, and introduced myself to Mr. Davenport, of the Howard Athenæum—of course under my new name, " Captain *Morton Price.*" Both gentlemen tendered me engagements, and both said it was of no use my going to New York. To both I said, " Why ?"—and both replied, with a mysterious shake of the head, " I guess an English amateur will not get supported *there,* any ways !" This discouraging communication I forthwith entrusted to my friend, *Jacobus,* who, I needn't say, took great interest in my Transatlantic " spec." for his sagest consideration, and his reply was, " Oh, try it !" I did, and the result of the trial will be given anon.

We stayed but a few days in Boston, and in that time we got our eyes pretty considerably opened as to American habits, manners, customs ; to all of which we resolved not to subscribe more than was actually necessary, by which you will understand our first impressions were not of a favourable kind.   Doubtless many of my descriptions may seem to the Uninitiated, exaggerated.   Can't help it, and to all unbelievers, I say—Go, See, Come home again, and present me with a handsome testimonial, in consideration of my virtue as the most veracious of historians.

Provided with letters of introduction from *Jacobus*, and others whose acquaintance I had made in Boston, to a few supposed-to-be-influentials in New York, we started one fine morning for, and arrived one wet night at, the Empire City ; we went the whole way by rail, and our ideas of the vaunted comfort of American railway travelling was, together with our bodies, dreadfully shaken ere the termination of our day's travel.   Ample description of the carriages, conductors, *et posse comitatus*, will be hereafter found in the course of this admirable work, and when found will, I dare say, be " *made a note*" of, as therein will be contained much necessary information to those who grudge paying first-class fare in England, and consider second-class carriages uncomfortable.

CHAPTER IV.

NEW YORK.

" So this is New York, waiter, eh ?" I facetiously *inquired* of an intelligent, but somewhat greasy specimen of black humanity, who, napkin on arm, was mentally measuring my Banker's account, as he waited behind me at breakfast, in an enormous unpleasant-smelling apartment of the Metropolitan Hotel. It is wonderful how apt these woolly-wooden heads are at " counting a fellah up," and their courtesy or contempt becomes accordingly soon manifest His reply, " Guess it's nothing else," came gravely from his lips, as he arranged the never-ending little dishes all round me, and politely added, " Tea or Coffee, sah ?" My answer, " Mix them," brought a grin to his old mug, which suddenly assumed a most deferential tinge, as on looking up, I perceived Lucille had entered the room, and was making her way towards us ; to accomplish which, she had to tack down one side, then bout ship, up the centre, and finally " wear" round something that looked like a young steam engine, but which *was* a stove.

Darkie was all alive—he couldn't conceal his admiration ; and when she addressed him with a smiling " Good morning," he fairly rubbed his hands in glee, and said he would have the " Honah to attend us while we stayed." He said his name was " *Parkah*, Missa Parkah—yes, sah, and what would the young lady take, &c." They are the queerest beings, but I am not going to make *this* a black chapter anyhow. We had a nice suite of apartments looking out on to the Broadway—*the* Broadway ! that once I heard Henry Russell, or some one else say, was fifty miles long by five wide, or something equally approaching the truth. (My Yankee readers will here say, " He'll be pitching into our Broadway, you'll see !")

Looking on the Broadway from the hotel windows, the most remarkable of remarkables thereon are the omnibuses ; looking from the street

itself, the irregularity and unequalness of the buildings first strike the
eye. (" Go it, stranger!") All the tops of the omnibuses are white, and
this being a hottish morning, numbers of them had large umbrellas,
under which the driver sat. They (the omnibuses) have no conductor,
each passenger, on entering, pays through a hole in the roof. Six cents
will take you anywhere the "bus" goes; but you can't ride outside
anyhow—there are no fittings for that luxury. Everybody hang their
heads and arms out of the windows, and look very hot, and the equine
progress is nearly as rapid as our own institution of that ilk at home.
Lucille amused herself, one entire morning, in sketching the drivers'
hats! If hats are not liable to duty, I shall bring home a box full of
specimens for presentation to my numerous low-comedian friends.   I
have said our windows faced the Broadway, and snugly seated at one of
the said windows, I chronicled my first impressions of the frequenters
of the said Broadway.

From nine until twelve, *the* street seems well filled with a well-
dressed number of people, evidently out for shopping purposes;
carriages are numerous (when I say carriages, I mean vehicles—New
York is not yet *quite* Paris, London, Dublin, or St. Petersburg, in the
matter of carriages) ; crinoline moderate, and cash evidently plenty.
This crowd, panorama-like, passes away, and from twelve to three *the*
street is comparatively deserted, which fact renders the appearance of
individuals more interesting. This appearance generally shapes itself
in that of *man ;* few of the softer sex making their appearance at this
time of day ; hence, one would imagine I should have little to say
respecting dress, manners, &c., &c. Not so. New York, just now, is
full of strangers and visitors ; thence comes my first cause for exclamation—(my pet one, stolen from——never mind whom), " Great Nature !"

Americans in New York, unlike Englishmen in London, are to be
" counted up" by the cut of their clothes. It would be no easy matter
for the cleverest of cockneys to say correctly, " *That* is a Yorkshire
gentleman, *that* an Irish, *that* a Scotch, or Welsh," though he would,
without difficulty, " spot" a Frenchman, or German ; but your New

Yorker will "guess" the birthplace of every one of his own countrymen he meets *on* Broadway, and, at the present time of writing, my experience having enlarged itself since first jotting down these notes, I think I could do, two out of five.   Five!—yes, dear reader, *five*.   How many sorts, in the name of wonder, are there ?

Well, I don't know, but I'll give you a few of them.   There are the Down Easters (Bostonites), Connecticut Yankees, Southerners (Kentuckians), the F. F. V.'s. South Carolinians and North do. (supposed to be the meanest people in the world), Georgians, Pennsylvanians, Creoles, Louisianians, Alabamas, Mississipians, New Jerseyites, Texans, Californians, Pike's Peak rowdies, the Illinois, and Indiana suckers, to say nothing of the Bowery bo-hoys and ga-hals, and Broadway swells, *cum multis aliis*—all differing as widely in character and costume as a Kaffir from a Christian.   This motley lot usually condense themselves inside the ground-floor windows, and outside and around the doors of Hotels, Boarding Houses, &c., ever and anon taking a stroll down and up the Broadway to stretch their legs, and stare any stray pretty girl out of countenance.   They, however, are not worse in *that* line than our own Club Loafers ; indeed, the first named are, perhaps, the better of the twain.   These, about four o'clock, become mingled with a rapidly increasing crowd of——well—of *females*. (Holloa, stranger, draw it mild !)

I arrived in New York, you must bear in mind, in May, 1859, and at that time a fashion existed of wearing an extent of hoops and crinoline, perfectly ludicrous ; I do not hesitate to say that had one of these ladies appeared in one of our English towns, the *gamins* would have had a fine chance ; however, time has passed, and so in a great measure has the enormity of this folly, but at the time of which we are inditing, there it was, in all its greatness, and Broadway was enveloped in the garments of Beauty.

Are the American ladies handsome ?

Well, *I guess* I have been in a good many countries "where Beauty most doth dwell," and I was never so struck with woman's *face* before ; but (hang those "buts") there are two sorts of beauty *on* Broadway—the beauty of Nature and the beauty of Art, and my mental exclamations of, " What a beautiful girl!" " What a well made-up woman !" will explain all that is necessary.   Ladies no longer possessed of the bloom of youth, and with little claim to maturer charms, go in at the hare's-foot, puff, paint pot, pearl powder, and Indian ink, with Vestris-like skill, and the uninitiated are dumbfoundered at their brilliance. *We* of the Green-room (ahem !) know it at a glance—however, the loveliness of American women, " without paint," is an institution of itself, and I bow at its shrine.

Broadway is misnamed—it should rather have been called *Long*way, for the pavements are narrow, and the road in no part more than 40ft. or 50ft. wide.   The shops, or *stores* as they are called, are magnificent in appearance ; there is nothing in Regent-street equal to numbers in Broadway.   I propose, *before* I shut my book, describing the cost and method of building *a marble store.*

Who, that is theatrically inclined or acquainted, has not heard and read of the name of Brough ? Alas ! one of that name, since my return to England, has by his death caused many an enemy to the Profession and Professional writers, to point the finger of unchristian contempt at Professional want of thrift, Professional carelessness of the morrow, Professional dislike to purchasing the Provisional Parachute for the Professional rainy day.

With William Brough, of Brooklyn's special permission, I beg to introduce him to you, reader. William Brough, uncle to the " *Brothers Brough*," a naturalised Yankee, and confirmed Englishman, withal a good fellow, called on me soon after we arrived ; *Jacobus* had written to him, as being one thoroughly "*posted*" in all theatrical matters, and who would, and could, put me in the path to fame, and——winning my wager.   I found him a *treat* ; full of anecdote, fond of Whisky in moderation, and awfully addicted to Gout.   We went into business as quickly as possible.   I found that New York, as far as theatricals were concerned, was rapidly going out of town, and dull as the proverbial ditch-water.   There was but one theatre " The Metropolitan" (now called the Winter Garden), where we could get an appearance, which we shortly arranged with the then lessee, Mr. C., to take place on Monday, May 22nd.

We were to take half the house after the deduction of a certain sum for expenses. And here, oh my English brethren and *followers*, let me warn you, should the insanity of supposing you can do better in America than in your own country, seize upon your disordered mind, and you follow your bent, beware of "*sharing houses.*" Be you clever as you may, be your Houses, as they should be—"All *orders*, my dear Sir," or "Madam," will be the manager's response to all pecuniary inquiries. You have no redress, no alternative, but to take what he gives you ; and if you are independent, throw up the engagement, or if otherwise, play upon the same *complimentary* terms.

We played on Monday, Tuesday, and Wednesday to average houses in my own operetta, *All's Fair in Love and War, Delicate Ground, Perfection,* and *Loan of a Lover.* We were *called* each night, and my Epilogue met with a most flattering reception, but (oh, those *buts* again !) the Press, to a man, cut *me* up—*apropos* of which, I must narrate a little incident. On the first night after I had played in the operetta, and *Delicate Ground,* feeling myself somewhat *dry,* I went round to a restaurant, near the Theatre, and while imbibing a "*cocktail,*" the following question and answer met my ears, and at once, amused and disgusted me :—

"Have you been into the Met ? I hear this Captain is not so bad."

"Not I," spoken thickly ; "I'm not going to write critiques upon Amateurs. I guess he won't get much out of me."

In a few moments an acquaintance came in and forthwith introduced me to the last speaker, "Mr. Wiggins, of ' The Trumpeter' newspaper." Mr. W., looked stupidly surprised, and *did* publish a critique the reverse of complimentary—*hinc illæ lachrymæ*—" fair play *is* a jewel, but *not* Mr. W's motto. "The General," a leading paper, did me the honor of criticising me as follows. The italics are my own.

" Captain Price announces himself as ' an Amateur,' very unwisely, we think, as he is not good enough player to overbalance that Amateur impression, and *the really good points of acting he developes* are lost sight of by *an audience prepared to expect* crudeness and less than mediocrity - - - - - In certain parts of his playing of *Citizen Sangfroid he deserves warm applause, and receives it.*"

" Captain Morton Price obeyed an enthusiastic call at the conclusion of the piece, and spoke a witty and novel Epilogue, which was well received. However, playgoing folk *are a little shy of amateurs,* &c., &c." —*Tribune.*

Turn we now to more pleasanter matter. Lucille became a favorite with her audience the moment she appeared, and succeeded in eliciting from some of the coldest houses we had the misfortune to play to, unmistakeable applause. Feeling, in the ignorance of our hearts, that we had made a success, we invested any number of cents in the purchase of newspapers. Judge then of the state of my appetite when I perused such ill-natured and discrepant notices as the following :—

" The gentleman cánnot be said to possess brilliant histrionic talents, but he is an *exceedingly* pleasing, agreeable actor, and sings with much taste. The lady is decidedly clever, and cannot fail becoming a great favorite." Again, " The Captain obeyed a unanimous complimentary call, and thereupon spoke an amusing doggrel Epilogue, which excited great attention and applause ; *in the main he did not ' hit.' *"

In justice to my fair coadjutor, I will here extract the following compliment to herself from the *Express :*—

" Miss Lucette is an artist of extraordinary promise ; she is very young, very pretty—a pure English blonde, with a mass of that peculiar blonde hair so seldom seen in perfection in this country, and quite natural and unaffected in her acting. The *Tribune* was right in saying that she made the most perfect success achieved here for many years by an English actress."

On the Wednesday night I ventured to inquire what the *business* was like ; and received for my reply, " No money !" I asked my informant, who was my friend Brough, to " be kind enough to say that again," and on his doing so, " Up sticks !" was the order ; and without our illustrious names in the bills, the *honorable* lessee played to empty benches for the remainder of the week, and was obliged to shut up shop.

Such was the ending of our beginning—"flat, stale, and unprofitable"—very ; and I should have been off to try other fields but for a little accident, which I will here narrate, for the (as usual) benefit of all whom it may concern.

When I left Boston, I distinctly remember placing a £50 Bank of England Note in my writing-desk, keeping in my pocket-book sufficient for travelling and current expenses. Three weeks since then, had now elapsed, and my Hotel Bill was presented, which amounted to three hundred and eighty-eight dollars. Gemini !—seventy-seven pounds sterling, for three persons and a servant for three weeks, taking all our meals at the *table d'hôte* with the οι πολλοι. Turn back for the name of the Hotel, reader, and "when found, make a note of it." However, I thought I might just have enough to clear out, when after a minute search (during which, palpitation of the heart predominated) in every nook and corner of the said desk, I discovered that my only friend, the £50 note, had vanished ! Without communicating the sad bereavement to our little circle, I immediately went to the office, and inquired for one of the numerous proprietors of the Hotel, who appeared in the form of a half man, half boy (what I have heard termed a hobble-de-hoy), a boy in years and countenance—a man in dress and impudence ; and having explained the circumstances, stating that I could get any amount I wanted from England by return mail, I was cut short with, " Well, I guess you had better look up your friends (*my friends !*), get the dollars right away, and clear out." Indignant at this sucking landlord's impertinence, I requested him to send his largest relative to me, which having done, and obtaining from him a modified, yet sufficiently annoying, answer, I forthwith sought the countenance of my friend Brough, who, in an interview with the assembled half dozen proprietors, offered to go security for the amount—himself being a householder and owner of property in Brooklyn. This was refused, and my monkey being thoroughly roused, their Yankee landlordships got such a wordy warming, as they have not yet forgotten, and Captain Morton Price is a thorn in their side to this day, as he promised to be. This matter was clinched by my giving them a cheque on my English bankers, and depositing in their hands *tangible* property to the value of some three times the amount of their abominable bill.

My revenge came, when, some four weeks after, the cheque being duly honoured, they had to return the goods and chattels, and their rival landlords in the city had a hearty laugh at the over-*smartness* of the Messrs. Lowband.

During our stay of some seven weeks in New York, of course I had much time to study the ways, means, habits and haunts of nearly every grade of society but as Fate ordained that I was to return to New York, and spend a yet longer period amid the turmoil of the overgrown young Mammoth, I reserve what I fear will be a lengthy notice (my gracious ! New York *is* a great place !) until I get back again, and hurry my reader on (hurrah !), who is anxious to know what I did next ?

Well, next——but wait a bit ; I have one little anecdote to relate, before we leave New York, yet. A certain (or, as the sequel proved, an uncertain) Dr. Ward having been engaged during some twelve years of his existence in writing, and getting written, composing and having composed, an opera, unfortunately for us just as we were preparing for our northern flight, arrived at *its* termi*nation* and *his* determi*nation* of its represen*tation* for the gratifi*cation* of his friends, and a do*nation* towards a Fund for the Rescue of Certain Lands, Hereditaments, &c., y'clept *Mount Vernon*, wherein are supposed to repose the mortal remains of, I believe, the immortal Washington (upon my word I am not *sure*)—he, Ward (not Washington) had heard and seen Lucille in our operetta, and immediately conceived that she, in conjunction with Miss Lucy Escott, and a Miss Adelaide Phillips (three prima donnas !) would form a galaxy of talent that must carry the thing "*right away.*" It seems that Miss Phillips and all the gentlemen engaged (among the latter was one Dr. Guilmette) I merely mention this that should a certain celebrated English tenor chance to read this he may know that his *Homœopathic adviser* still liveth, and his iniquities are known to the writer, had long since been well up in the music of this Doctor's opera, and of course they were far ahead of Lucille in the business ; however, after some demur, the latter agreed to get up in it in consideration of 50 dols. per night, for three nights certain. The time came, the house was three parts full, the opera was played, Lucille *obtained the only two encores* in the evening ; the Doctor was called, the curtain rose, and the whole Corps Operatique were discovered *en tableau.* The

Doctor made a speech, in which he thanked the entire company individually from first to last, the big drum and the call-boy, and—*omitted* Lucille! I was standing at the wing nearly suffocating with rage, the Doctor was bowing himself off, the curtain was about to descend, the audience were applauding, the——well, I don't know how she did it, but when I had done winking and rubbing my eyes, there she stood, *Lucille stood,* curtseying to her audience, and apparently, with her finger and thumb screwing a small piece of earthly clay out of the wonder-stricken Doctor's sinister arm, she said, " Doctor, you have forgotten *me !"*

A whirlwind of applause followed this pithy reminder; the Doctor, speechless with surprise, looked on bewildered, as, turning to the audience, the young lady (whom I didn't think could have cried, " Boh! to a goose") said—

" Ladies and Gentlemen, I have had but a few days to get up in the music of this opera, and I should be sorry indeed to think that the Doctor's silent condemnation of my endeavours should meet with your approval."

No occasion to say more, thought I; and none there was, I never heard a more decided negative to an opinion, than was given by that audience to that Doctor. The Press took it up on the following day, and I cannot refrain from giving one or two quotations from some of the leading papers :—

" Miss Lucette, in Dr. Ward's speech after the opera, was passed over unnoticed (whether intentionally or accidentally we know not), whilst the composer complimented the different artists; but in our humble opinion no one contributed more to the enjoyment of the audience than this clever girl, who sang her part charmingly, and whose sweet voice and fascinating style were among the chief attractions of the evening."—*Dispatch.*

" After the opera the composer was called before the curtain, and thanked the various performers for the interest they had taken in the production of his work. He quite *forgot* to say a good word for Miss Lucette, whose performance was one of the most interesting features of the evening, so that energetic young lady made a pretty little speech on her own account, and the Doctor then repaired his neglect by publicly acknowledging his indebtedness to her, and the audience dispersed in the best possible humour."—*Leader.*

Some of the papers were even more severe, and whether owing to this little contretemps, or that the success of the opera was equivocal, I know not, but it was withdrawn, and though we and others stayed a whole fortnight in New York solely on Dr. Ward's account, that gentleman refused point-blank to pay any of the artists more than one night's salary. No redress, no satisfaction, no anything, but to grin and bear it; so that had *I* been engaged in its representation, I should have had to have scored a loss; as it was, no great harm was done as regarded my wager; Lucille pocketed the 50 dols., and we turned our thoughts upon packing up and departing.

This anecdote I have related that unbelievers may have their faith in American encouragement of English artists somewhat shaken, and to warn them of the necessity of having their salary, or at least one half of it, in advance.

After having seen as much as I could afford to see of New York, and made notes thereon for your benefit, good reader, and my conscience, and my funds having been recruited, and my second Hotel bill being paid, *apropos*, of which I beg to state that I can recommend No. 767, Broadway, the European Hotel, kept by some people (a cross between French and German, and very worthy withal). No pretension outside (the House, I mean), but most comfortable within, Mr. Hartmann, the proprietor, is a very fair artist, and has a Studio, on Broadway, leaving the feminine portion of the establishment to take care of the same, and to those ladies, mother and daughter, I here tender my mite of gratitude for their uniform kindness to our party during our sojourn at No. 767 ; *and* having determined on my route, we started for Boston " bock agin"—by steam-boat this time, our destination being Quebec, and a pleasant trip we had to Portland, part of the way by water, the rest by land.

Brough accompanied us to Boston, and with him I left the manuscript of an entertainment* (my first attempt at anything of the kind),

---

* *The Double Courtship*, which, though trifling in construction, was lucky enough to draw for us audiences, of various sorts and sizes, at more than eighty representations.—M. P.

which I had employed my leisure moments in New York in writing, thinking that from what I had seen and heard of American reception of, and encouragement to, English talent (ahem !) in legitimate Drama, I might stand a better chance in Halls and Concert Rooms than in Theatres. This Entertainment, however, was either not printed, or did not reach us, until we arrived at Montreal, and many blessings did our friend Brough and his printer get from the lips and hearts of Lucille and myself, for the delay.

CHAPTER V.

QUEBEC.

QUEBEC is a city built on a rock, &c., &c., (*vide* Handbook), and a mighty tall rock, too, only about 350 feet above the level of the river. How on earth Wolfe and his army ever got up to the top is a wonder. No man with any other *name* could have done it, I believe. However, any one who wishes to know, when and how, and where it *was* done, wont get any information from *me*, for lots of writers, ere now, have described (from each other's descriptions) all about it, and having myself read it, and wrote it so very early in life, that I have totally forgotten all the principal parts of the performance, I will omit the History of Quebec, and continue my own.

We went by steamer from Boston to Portland, a dreadfully dismal, unfinished sea-port town, " way down in Main," withal the eastern terminus of the Grand Trunk Railway, and the talked-of destination of that floating Mammoth, the " Great Eastern" steamship, though what on earth, or rather *water*, she'll do when she gets there, no one can opine; there are no warehouses for her merchandise, and no hotels for her passengers. However, that sensible body of gentlemen, mis-named her directors, I suppose know best, though an intelligent Yankee told me " there was no reason on ' airth' why she shouldn't go to New York, as there was water enough in the Hudson to float " six such as she," and deducting the odd five, I believe him.

We had our first experiences of the Grand Trunk Railway from this place to Quebec, or rather to Point Levi, and they did not please us; but as railway travelling is the same all over Canada, I will describe it elsewhere, and my readers must be content, for the present, to embark with us in a rickety old steamer, to cross, for the first time, the great St. Lawrence River, which between Point Levi and Quebec is some three miles wide.

It was nearly nine in the evening when we drove up to the door of Russell's Hotel, having been thither recommended by Brough; and weary, dirty, aching in every bone, Lucille, for the first time since starting, in an execrable humour *for her*—Stocks (my man), perfectly used up with tobacco-smoke, dust, and his endeavours to " keep things straight"—we looked forward to a " cumfy" supper, and a ten-hour turn-in with unmitigated pleasure.

Judge ye our intense misery on being informed that they were all full !—and they wouldn't or couldn't tell you where to go. Lucille was looking really ill.

" Would the ladies like to sit in the drawing-room ?"

" Of course, they would—anywhere ;" and to the drawing-room they went, while the wretched Stocks and I hunted up the town for quarters, which we at last found in an Americau House. The landlord was not to be found ; but his deputy, a dissipated-looking cross between a billiard-marker and a pot-boy showed me some comfortable apartments, which I instantly secured, ordered supper, fetched Lucille, who I found undergoing the agony of being stared out of countenance by the assem-bled female portion of the Russell-House boarders ; and after worrying some hard-boiled eggs, and some soft-boiled chickens, we all tumbled in, tired to death.

*   *   *   *   *   *

We are at breakfast—bad coffee, bad eggs, bad everything, but our temper—which having been *so* bad over-night, could not well be worse, is of the twain, improved. Besides, we are in Canada—our own country, her Majesty's dominions, and feel ourselves Englishmen again. We shall have respect shown us, and *our rooms* to ourselves.

Shall we ?

" Guess you'll find these rooms pretty comfortable !"

Now there was no reason why anyone should " guess" otherwise, from outward appearances, therefore the " guess" causing a simultaneous clatter of dropped knives and forks, and an ejaculation of " Gracious !" may at first cause surprise. Read on. We had been indulging in a good loud laugh at Lucille's sudden discovery that what looked outwardly a good egg, inwardly wasn't, when like—nothing else in language, this question, (or rather assertion, for " guessing" has a different meaning here to that which Walker assigns it), burst upon us, and, raising our eyes, red with tears of merriment, we saw—an individual. Yes, an un-invited individual, seated on a chair near the door, his legs stretched to their full extent over the carpet, and arms, ditto, into the pockets of the encasement of said legs.

After a slight pause, and unflinching sustainment of the concentrated gaze of three pairs of astonished eyes, the guessing individual repeated his guess, adding however emphatically, " Darn'd sight comfortabler than you'd have got down *thar !*" (with a kick of his right ·leg towards the door—a wink of his right eye, and jerk of his right thumb over his right shoulder, simultaneously aiding and abetting the same.)

'Twas the landlord, a shock-headed, shocking ugly, shabby-looking Yankee.

" Landlord, I suppose," I said, politely.

" Guess I am," (moving himself and chair, and taking up position immediately on my left flank, and nodding to the ladies, who were rapidly getting " used up" in their efforts to restrain a roar).

·" Well now, have you *concluded* to stay ?"

" That depends upon circumstances," I replied.

" Twelve dollars be too much ?"

" A day ?"

A nod.

" Well, rather !"

" Piano," (a jerk towards something like a shut-up Bagatelle Board.) " Ladies play, I guess."

" Oh, yes, so do I." I replied, rising, ostensibly to try the instrument, but really to escape the monster's *breath—rum and onions !* Awful !

" Wretchedly out of tune," passing my fingers over the old-dog's-teeth-like-looking-ivory.

" Well now, that's odd. My darter plays on it first-rate—that's a fact !"

" You have daughters, have you ?" asked Lucille.

" He'er, Sa-rah (pronounced Sa-rare), come up !" shouted this strange mortal, without moving from his chair.

Sarah didn't require telling to " Come *up*," for she was " *up*" already, and came in, instanter ; and pertly nodding to the party collectively, sat *herself* down on the sofa, her *hoop* flying up as she did so, and displaying her legs as high as—where her garters ought to have been, but were *not*.

" Piano out of tune ?" said the father.

" Sure, *I* don't know," replied the daughter, with a toss of the head, and staring Lucille out of countenance.

Seeing impudence in the daughter's face and ignorance in the father's, I thought it time to send in a shot, so said, " Ah ! you are not the one who plays."

" Don't know no other," was the response.

" Well, then," I said, shutting up the instrument, " were I your music master, I should teach you the difference between in and out of tune—that is, if you have any ear for music. If you have, as I am bound to suspect, *none*, I wouldn't teach you at all."

The young lady transferred the favour of her stare to me, and rising in rage, said to her respected parent, " If you want me, I'm down stairs !"

(Exit Sa-rare.)

" Guess you've riled the young woman. She's terrible high—she is," half soliloquized the parent. " But touching them dollars ?" he immediately inquired.

The ladies by this time were fairly embarked in one uncontrollable fit of laughter, and retired under plea of unpacking.

A bargain (?) eventually was struck for 11 dols. a day, and the use of the Bagatelle—that is, Piano, to be tuned at landlord's expense.

We had scarcely shaken ourselves into our places, when Captain Bayly, of the Canadian Rifles, was announced, and in he came, his merry face illuminating the dingy room with a temporary ray of comic sunshine. Those of my readers who remember him on board the outward-bound ship, will imagine how glad we were to find him in Quebec. He had only lately been transferred with his Company from Toronto. In less than no time it was arranged that he should assist us on our " First appearance in Canada;" but how, and in what, required great consideration. The number of plays, in which there are but three or four characters, is so limited, and our stock comprising only *Delicate Ground*, and another (my Entertainment had not yet arrived from Boston, and even had it, we could not have made it available), I was perforce obliged to consent to write something " *right away*," in which the varied talent of Lucille, the Captain, and myself might be exhibited. Ten days, I thought, would suffice for the execution

of our project, for puffing, posting, and all other proclamation of
our arrival and intentions. My peregrinations in and around, and
experiences of, Quebec during that time, I will briefly record.

Quebec is at all times a dull-looking place, excepting when some
political row breaks out, which is but of rare occurrence, and unfortunately nothing of the kind took place while I was there, therefore, I
have no excitement to chronicle. Driving to Lorette, misnamed an
Indian village, for the *Indians* therein all speak French, and dress-like
the denizens of a mining district in England,—the Falls of Mont-
morenci (which are fully described by writers better able to do it than
I am*) and other sights within reasonable distance,—playing at Bowls
(there's a capital Alley opposite Russell's Hotel, kept by a very civil
fellow, named Bellereve, and much patronised by the officers of the
Garrison),—or Rackets (there's a tolerably good court, barring its
being made of wood, adjoining the Bowling Alley, but of which you
must be made a member, honorary or otherwise, before you can play),—
exploring the citadel and its cavernous communications, (which you
can't do without you know somebody who can give you leave),—or
listening to the band of the 39th, then quartered in Quebec, now in
Bermuda, playing in what is called the Governor's Gardens, (very unlike
most governor's gardens, unless indeed it be those of that stern governor
mentioned in the doleful ditty of " Villikins and his Dinah,") comprised the whole of my day-time pastime. The kindness of some of
the officers procured me many a dinner, not at my own expense, at
the city and elsewhere, and a game at Loo, or rubber of Whist, was a
real treat ; especially on one occasion, which, as a detail of the same
may be of use to beginners at the last-named charming game, I must
here narrate. I was one evening playing Whist at the Artillery mess.
Our party consisted of Lieut. Smith, Captain Brown, Major Robinson,
and myself. During the evening I had opportunities of discovering
that I knew more about the game than my military friends. They
didn't think so, and my " *asking for trumps*" was looked upon as a
downright " questio vexata"—a non-permissible declaration—a " do."
I thought of the time it had taken me to learn *how* to do it. I thought
of the looks, the laughs, the lashings I had received from thee, oh,

---

* " Weld's Vacation Tour in the United States and Canada," I recommend.

" Ingenui vultus puer !", my early instructor in the art of taking tricks, my *honor-able* friend, I thought of——but it was no use thinking. I cast a w(*h*)istful glance upon mine enemies, and kept my high cards in and played my low ones out—aye, with king, queen, and lots of little ones. Well, the night was gone and morning waned, when the Major being my opponent and dealer got confused as to where he had dealt last. He immediately commenced to count the cards left in his hands undealt.   The following dialogue resulted between us :

I. " Major, you can't do that."

MAJOR. " I beg your pardon, I can." (Da Capo with voluntary and involuntary . variations, the whole strength of the assembled chorus assisting the Major, my *bar* being a solo, my partner not succeeding in making it, as he ought to have done, a duetto).

I. " I'll bet you anything you like about it."

MAJOR. " What will you bet ?"

I. " I'll lay you ten pounds to five."

MAJOR. " Done !" (dealing on).   " Perhaps (with a wink to chorus), you would like to have a little more about it ?"

I. (getting savage) " Certainly, I will ; but you musn't deal !"

MAJOR (coolly) " Musn't I ? Why ?" (turning up the trump).

I. " Because, unless my partner plays dummy, you can't finish the game.   *I* shall not play any longer with players quite ignorant of the laws of the game."

MAJOR. " Oh, are we ?   Gentlemen, it is high time to leave off."

I. " High time."

MAJOR. " Perhaps you would like to lay a little more ?"

I. (thoroughly roused) " I'll lay you fifty pounds to ten !"

MAJOR. (wonderfully self-possessed) " Thank you, you shall.   Won't you play the game out ?"

I. " Certainly not."

MAJOR. " Then we claim the rubber !" (Pleasant laughter).

I. " Claim as you like, sir, but not until you have proved me wrong."

MAJOR. " I somehow think that will soon be done.   But first, to prove how little I think of your chance of being right, I will lay you an even hundred pounds I win the bets already made."

I. " You are positive ; so am I.   Done !

Voice at my elbow, " What a fool you are, the Major knows everything."

I. " Does he ?   He doesn't look like it !" (Sotto voce).

Pen, ink, and paper are produced in no time.   I find my name appended to a document assigning away from myself and heirs the sum of one hundred and sixty pounds to a party I never saw before, or heard of, and Major R.'s ditto, ditto, from himself and heirs the sum of one hundred and fifty pounds to my use and benefit, should said party *be wrong*, on the other.

Well, thus much being settled to the Major's satisfaction, I was presently called on to name my referee or umpire.   I, without hesitation, gave the name of Mr. P——, one of the best esteemed names on the British Turf, and one I had often heard mentioned in Whist disputes, and with whom I was slightly acquainted personally. A shout was raised at this of " Why not name Cœlebs, or the Portland Club ; *we* never heard of Mr. P——"

This last assertion from a party professing Whist was too much, and fairly losing my temper, I shouted rather than exclaimed, " Not know— never heard of George P—— ?   Then, gentlemen, all I have to say is, I will argue no more.   I leave the decision of the bets, as far as I am concerned, to him and no other.   Name *your* umpire, Major, and I am off."

MAJOR. " I name the Portland Club."

" Very good," was my reply ; and so would have ended a simple dispute with a simple wager, but that suddenly, and from whence I know not, a book was put before my eyes, in which I read the following :

" *Misdeal.* 10.

" *The dealer may not touch the cards upon the table to ascertain an error ; but he is not prohibited from counting the undealt cards.*"

This was betting (as *they* thought) on a certainty, with a vengeance ! And this I, perhaps, somewhat too hotly, remarked upon.

I saw triumph in the Major's face—dismay in those who had secretly hoped that the Major did *not* " know everything."   I saw an " odd trick" being played, and in I went to win.

" You had the pull of me in having possession, and knowing the contents of this book," I said, glaring round.   " Now, if any of you have Pec (an old Eton word, signifying money) and pluck enough to double the bet of a hundred pounds even, I will say ' Done !' again, to it ; and that (a snap of my fingers) for Cœlebs, and those who back his authority !"

No response. They thought me a greater or less fool than themselves ; couldn't make up their minds ; and, I suppose, gave me the benefit (though as things happened, *they* reaped it) of the doubt.

The wager was decided by the Portland Club, of which Cœlebs is a member, in my favour, *which decision was confirmed and approved by my umpire*. Mr. George P——.

It was *five months* before I got the money, but I got it then, and so ended my first and last bet in Canada, on Whist.

There was a little Cricket going on also, and we occasionally went to the Plains of Abraham to see the old English game played ; and now and then, the representation reminded me of sunny " lords," old Lansdown, or the Canterbury meetings. There were handsome women, fine-looking men, and lots to eat and drink—a good Band, and moderately good play ;—nothing to go into fits about, but a sort of All Muggleton *mélange*. Altogether, one could find something to do, and Quebec was bearable for the ten days we had to pass, before our first " little go" in Canada came off.

Well, time rolled on, of course ; " Sa-rare" after many determined efforts to introduce her hoops and legs into the sitting-room, at inconvenient hours, voted us " stuck-up Britishers," and kept herself to herself, as far as *we* were concerned. Our landlord, after being asked by me, one day when he sat in our presence for half-an-hour, with his hat on, " If he had a cold in his head ?" never troubled us again ; so, barring that we could get nothing fit to eat and drink, we were pretty comfortable. I had heard nothing of my Boston publisher, or Mr. Brough, so that we had given up all hopes of playing *The Double Courtship*, and I had worked like a man at a vehicle for the introduction of ourselves and Captain Bayly, and had finished, and entitled it, *A Country Manager's Perplexities*. The plot was far from original, but the situations were *startlingly* new, and the dialogue of a most spirited description—at least, *I* thought so ; so did Lucille ; so did Bayly. Now for a bill, I copy it *in extenso*, and think, for a maiden effort, it was not a bad one.

MUSIC ⚜ HALL,

ST. LEWIS STREET.

CAPTAIN MORTON PRICE

Has the honor to announce that he will commence his

Theatrical Tour through Canada and the United States,

ON

MONDAY EVENING

NEXT, JULY 25th, WITH A

Musical Melange and Entertainment,

AT THE MUSIC HALL,

In which he will be assisted by

MISS CATHARINE LUCETTE,

The youthful Prima Donna of Drury Lane, London, and

CAPTAIN BAYLY,

Of the Royal Canadian Rifles, well-known in Amateur Circles, as the " Primo Buffo" of the celebrated A. B. C. Club, of which Captain Morton Price is the Founder.

The Entertainment will be under the immediate PATRONAGE of

Colonel Munro, C.B., Commandant, & the *Officers of the Garrison ;*

And by kind permission of the Commanding Officer, the

SPLENDID BAND OF THE 39th REGIMENT WILL ATTEND.

The DOORS will open at A QUARTER before EIGHT, and the Overture to William Tell will be commenced by *The Band*, at a quarter past, precisely. After which the Curtain will rise upon an Impromptu Sketch, drawn in a great hurry by Captain Morton Price, and entitled

"A COUNTRY MANAGER'S PERPLEXITIES."

SIGNORA MARITANA BALFERINA,—(a Prima Donna, Pretending to
　Pretensions) .... *Miss Catharine Lucette.*

PROFESSOR HOPSKOTCH,—a high-low comedian and rising young
　Acrobat, pretending to do everything) .... *Captain Bayly.*

THE MANAGER,—Slightly deranged, from ill management ...... *Captain Morton Price,*

Who begs to assure "Ladies and Gentlemen" that there is no real cause for alarm in the following *apparently* Alarming (considering the size of the Stage), Announcement,

During the Evening, *Captain Bayly will introduce a Daring Feat of*

EQUESTRIANISM,

Never before attempted in this Country ! ! ! And in the Course of the entertainment, the following SONGS, &c., will be sung :—

LA BRINDISI, (from Traviata) .... *Miss Catharine Lucette.*

ECHO DUETT, (from Guy Mannering).................... *Miss Lucette & Captain Price.*

VILLIKINS, (Buffo Songs)............................. *Captain Bayly.*

THERR BE NONE OF BEAUTY'S DAUGHTERS (original)........ *Captain Morton Price.*

MA BELLE FRANCE (from La Fille du Regiment).......... *Miss Lucette.*

PART FROM THEE, NEVER (original)...................... *Miss Lucette & Captain Frice.*

THE YOUNG MAN FROM THE COUNTRY (buffo) .... *Captain Bayly.*

EVER OF THEE, (ballad, *by desire*) .... *Miss Catharine Lucette.*

After which an **OPERATIC SELECTION** will be performed by **THE BAND,** and the Evening Entertainment will conclude with a

MUSICAL MELANGE,

Ending with

"GOD SAVE THE QUEEN."

PRICES OF ADMISSION—Reserved Seats (secured without extra charge　··　⎫
　　Double Tickets for Lady and Gentleman　··　··　⎬ 75 Cents.
　　　　　Single Tickets　··　··　··　··　··　50 „
　　　　　Centre Galleries　··　··　··　··　··　50 „
　　　　　Side Galleries　··　··　··　··　··　25 „

Tickets and Seats to be secured of Mr. Wheeler, at the Music Hall, of Mr. Russell, Russell's Hotel, Mr. Purdy, the Metropolitan Hotel, Fabrique Street, and at Mr. Sinclair's Library.

VIVAT REGINA.

Quebec, July 21st, 1859.

My posters had, of course, been out a long time, but side by side with
them were those of the " Parodi Opera Troupe," which were playing on
the Thursday, Friday, and Saturday, *before us*, and on Tuesday and
Wednesday, *after*. This was decidedly a counter-attraction, and I was
horridly afraid that at our very onset we should have to write " failure."
A word or two here about the theatre, or more properly speaking,
" Music Hall," though, as either one or the other, it is a wretched contrivance. The rent is 40 dols. a night (£8 English), without a property
or assistance of any description, save that of a *money-taker* at night,
which is invariably embodied in the person of the man who has the
letting and charge of the Hall—an arrangement which, on my second
visit to Quebec, I peremptorily declined, to the evident chagrin of said
person ; more of which anon. I have now the pleasing task of recording
the great kindness of the Press generally of Quebec. Unlike that of
New York, they *could* see the possibility of a *gentleman* being an *actor,*
and their notices, before and after the performance, were couched in the
most generous terms.

I here extract, from the *Chronicle :*

" By reference to our advertising columns, it will be seen that two
stars have suddenly dropped upon the dramatic world of Quebec. A
Captain Morton Price and Miss Catharine Lucette, who propose giving
a dramatic and musical Entertainment in this city on Monday next,
under the patronage of the military. The Captain is an author, amateur actor, and composer of celebrity in England, and the young lady
made her *début,* as *prima donna,* at Drury Lane, London, last spring,
and occasioned quite a 'sensation.' A gallant officer of the Canadian
Rifles is also advertised to appear ; so, if our good folks need novelty
to draw them within the walls of the Music Hall, in good truth, they
have it now."

Night came ; few places had been secured, and it was with nervous
trepidation I, after dressing, reconnoitred the house through the thumb-
hole of the curtain. Joy ! It is all right ! The galleries filled, and
body of the hall filling fast. The band of the 39th, " by the kind permission of Colonel Munro," were in the orchestra, and the big drum
didn't beat louder than my heart, as I hurried to Lucille's dressing-
room, and bade her, " Be smart !" in all senses of the words. In ten
minutes we were at work.

And thus spoke the *Mercury* :

" Giving the lady the precedence, we pronounce Miss Catharine Lucette a most charming vocalist : her acting is graceful, lady-like, and withal *piquant.* The Captain has a pleasing and extraordinary high tenor voice, of which he is perfect master. As an actor, his coolness, knowledge of stage business, combined with great facial powers and volubility of speech, place him beyond criticism as an amateur."

We had over £50 in the Hall, which is a " fine house" for Quebec. This over, I turned my countenance towards Montreal, and after ascertaining that there were no end of concert rooms, halls, and a theatre therein, we did our packing, and found ourselves, in a few days, starting from Point Levi, by an afternoon train (having cleverly missed the morning one), for Longueil. The last-named place being to Montreal what Point Levi is to Quebec, the twain being the termini of the railroad from one to the other ; and each conveniently situated on the *wrong* side of the water (the River St. Lawrence)—that is, should you wish to visit either of the cities, which the chances are you do, when you are travelling for no other purpose.

Wood and water, water and wood, wretched hovels, squalid people, dirty children, mangy pigs, and emaciated cattle are all you'll see in the dreary length between the Scylla and Charybdis of Quebec and Montreal. Not one cheering ray of excitement throughout the entire journey ; therefore, having nothing else to write about, I will give you a description of the train.

They are all the same throughout Canada and the United States ; so peruse this carefully—I shall treat of them no more. Our own first-class carriages cannot be termed outwardly attractive ; but when you open the door and look in, the interior is cosy, comfortable, and almost luxurious. Those I am writing of are like large caravans, some 40 feet long, and not like the English ones, divided into three compartments. They have a door at each end, and a platform ; by means of which you can pass from, to, and *through* every carriage in the train ; your first peep into a moderately full one is not assuring of comfort ; very narrow, with passage down the centre, and seats accommodating (?) two persons each side ; I have counted forty-four people in one carriage. Their speed seldom attains the rate of 25 miles per hour. The conductors generally are civil fellows, but fearfully off-hand—a manner engendered by the heterogeneous medley of mankind with whom they have to treat and converse. They have a curious word of command for summoning the passengers in and out of the trains—viz., "All aboard!" and "All ashore!" This, I discovered, after many inquiries, originated in the fact that before the Grand Trunk Railroad was invented, all traffic was by barges on the canals which formerly extended almost the entire length, east and west, of Canada, and these were the captains' words of command ; and the said captains, oddly enough being, in many cases, on the conclusion of the railroad, transmogrified into railway guards and conductors, retained their nautical vocabulary. Wood is used instead of coal, and the nuisance from the " *smuts*" is intolerable. Oh, my friends!—female and otherwise—bear in mind should you travel these regions, take with you, as your constant companion, a *dark coloured* wrap-rascal, of a *texture* similar to that worn by gentlemen on the Derby day. It will save you a mint of money in soaps and garments—folds into the smallest compass, and will not inconvenience you with heat. Ladies should have a hood of the same. Never mind the look of the thing! Lucille's head, on one or two occasions, when she took off her bonnet, reminded me of some illustrations I have seen devised by certain " wonderful hair-dye" inventors as advertisements.

Another word of advice, while I'm i' the vein : always carry your own larder and wine-cellar with you. You will get nothing to eat or drink on the way, but the vilest of compounds, and no time to stow them. A cup of tea, if you don't sit down to drink it, is 25 cents ; aud a bottle of beer—ugh! (Bass, Allsop, hear me!) 50 ditto.

As we neared our destination, a terrific thunder-storm overtook us ; and never do I remember such lightning. The storm seemed to travel with us, and whether we were really going faster than usual I know not, but the sensation was that of being borne along by the powers of the storm, independent of steam agency, while the combined noises of wind, rain, and thunder, and the rattling of the train itself were deafening. Reader, you have *dreamed* what is beyond my power to describe ; so have I. It was horrible ! The passengers were frightened.

" Say, stranger !—this licks anything you have seen in your country, any way ?"

This remark came from a man—of course, an American—just after a flash had so blinded me, that I had to pass my hand across my eyes to relieve the pain.

" Well," I answered, " I don't think I ever saw such lightning in *any* country ; and I don't care ever to see it again.   It is too close to be pleasant."

" Yes, it's just sorter thing makes a fellar think thar's not much use in dollars.   Don't it, now ?"

(Curiously expressed, I thought, but *good*, notwithstanding.)

" Make a bad man wish he were a better one, may be," I said.

" Young lady frightened ?" he asked, in a rough-kind-way.

" Rather."

" Tender critturs, women.   No nation use in a storm.   Thunder ! Thar's a blinder !   We whips the world for storms, *we* does !"

I really think our companion considered that *he* had something to do with the uproar of the elements, and was glorified thereby.

We ran through it, or it outran us in about half an hour, and a glorious moon lit up the bright *metal* roofs of Montreal, as we steered into the station ; and, having got there safely, so endeth this Chapter.

CHAPTER VI.

MONTREAL.

MONTREAL, ladies and gentlemen, is an island, or rather, the city of Montreal is *situated* on an island.   The Rivers Ottowa and St. Lawrence rolling their rival lengths on either side, with hands across at either end, in the shape of two estuaries, the names of which I never inquired, so don't know. The city of Montreal, as viewed by me with one eye, the other being under the influence of one of the before-mentioned obnoxious " *smuts*," appeared a most unsatisfactory and unsatisfied sort of a city. Unlike Quebec, the streets are well arranged and dreadfully *holy* (N.B. there's a church or chapel in nearly all of them—three-fourths being Roman Catholic, the remainder, all sorts; and McAdam being wholly unknown).

The houses are large and small—two factions in short ; no sliding-scale, except in the winter months, which are seven in the twelve, when all situations in Canada are slippery in the extreme. The principal hotels, of which there are but two, are enormous edifices, the others mere pot-houses. The principal streets, of which there are but two, are wide and hand-some, the rest mere lanes. The people, of whom there are but two, the rich, holding high estate, the poor, holding nothing. There is nothing *middling* in Montreal. One of the said two people, the high, are dissatisfied that they can't be higher; the other, the low, are striving to be lower; and it is probable that half a century will see them attain their object. Mind you, *all* of the foregoing is not a one-eyed view. Montreal is even more *Frenchy* than Quebec, and a stranger finds it hard to imagine himself under the sovereignty of H.G.M. the Queen. The magistrates, the merchants, and the money-lenders (who comprise the " upper Ten") are all French; and the laws are French, and the streets have got French names, and everybody speaks French.

We put up at the St. Lawrence Hall, a very fine hotel, or rather boarding-house (there is no such thing as an hotel on this side of the Atlantic ; and he who thinks to find one must make up his mind to be a long-shore Flying Dutchman, or Wandering Jew. The proprietors, Messrs. Hogan and Penn (since, Hogan solus, Penn having departed), are first-class providers, for both passers-by and permanent lodgers. I will here append a copy of the Bill of Fare, as presented for our inspection a few days after our arrival :—

SAINT LAWRENCE HALL,
MONTREAL.
BILL OF FARE.

THURSDAY, AUGUST 4th, 1859.

SOUP .. .. Maccaroni.

ENTREES .. Roguet Canellas. Rognon Sauté à Champagne.
Selmi de Canard. Beef Steak & Oyster Sauce.

JOINTS .. Roast Beef. Roast Venison. Boiled Chicken.
Boiled Leg of Mutton. Boiled Ham.

VEGETABLES .. Potatoes. Turnips. Parsnips.
Onions. Celery. Beets.

PASTRY .. Bread and Butter Pudding. Apple Tarts.
Claret Jelly. Whipped Cream. Mince Pies.

DESSERT .. Fruit. Cakes. &c., &c.

LIST OF WINES.

Madeira ....dols. 2.00	Champagne (Dry) Max Sauterne &	
Do. superior...............2.50	Co. Sillery ....dols. 2.50	
Do. East India.............3.00	Do. Max Sauterne & Co. Verzenay 2.50	
Sherry......................2.00	Do. do. pints .. 1.25	
Do. Pale 2.50	Do. Clicquot's 2.50	
Do. superior..............3.00	Do. do. pints 1.25	
Port.......................2.00	Moselle, Sparkling 2.50	
Do. Sandeman..............2.50	Do. Still 2.00	
Do. very old..............3.00	Hock, Sparkling...............2.50	
Champagne, English Moet, No. 1... 3.00	Do. Still 2.00	
Do. do. pints .. 1.50	Claret, Vin Ordinaire...........1.00	
Do. do. No. 2.. 2.50	Do. St. Julien 1.50	
Do. do. pints .. 1.25	Do. do. pints 0.75	
Do. Heidseick 2.50	Do: Chateau Margaux 2.50	
Do. do. pints........1.25	Do. Battaillie 2.50	
Do. Bouzy 2.50	Do. Chateau Lafitte 3.00	
Do. do. pints........1.25	Do. Sauterne...............1.50	
Do. Imported expressly for	Johannesberg, Prince Metternich's	
this establishment .. 3.00	Cabinet Wine.............. 4.00	
Do. Mumm's Cabinet 2.50	Burgundy 3.00	
Do. Mumm's Cabinet pints 1.25	Cider 0.75	
Do. Associates Verzeney.. 2.50	Do. pints....................0.37½	
Do. do. pints 1.25	Ale & Porter best brands 0.50	
Do. Ruinart's 2.50	Do. do. pints.... 0.25	

HOURS OF MEALS.

Breakfast from 8 to 10 o'clock. Dinner at Six o'clock.
Lunch from One to Two o'clock. Tea from Eight to Half-past Nine o'clock.
Dinner at Two o'Clock for those leaving by Afternoon Trains.
Dinner on SUNDAYS at Two o'Clock—Meals served in Rooms charged extra.
Children sitting at the Public Table will be charged full price.

NORDHEIMER'S MUSIC HALL.

This Evening, Captain Morton Price and Miss Lucette will appear.

THE WAITERS ARE PROVIDED WITH CARDS AND PENCIL.

Reads Englishy, doesn't it ?—and would eat all right, too, but for the messy American method of never letting you see the animal—that is, the joint of the animal, from which your "*helping*" is derived. A greasy nigger, down in some hidden slum, cuts up, picks, pats, and presents you with, in nine cases out of ten, the very fat, or lean, or raw, or over-done portion that you would have avoided had you witnessed the operation. I do like to *see* my " pound of flesh"—that's a fact.

To business. My readers will have observed that I had no agent in advance. Indeed, I considered the terms of my agreement did not comprehend my employing one ; and I was determined to avoid the slightest ground for quibble or controversy of any kind. This, however, was throughout my Canadian campaign, a serious drawback. It entailed the necessity of a sojourn in the town I intended performing in of four or five days, previously to opening ; and though the consequent expenses did not militate against the winning of the wager, they *did considerably* against the chance of my pecuniary benefit thereby.

Nordheimer is the name of the proprietor of the handsomest concert-hall in Canada. Remember it, my brethren, for good fellows are scarce, and he (Mr. Nordheimer), professionally or otherwise, is, in all senses of the term, one of the right sort. Liberal in his dealings, and assiduous in his attention, to which, through the good people of Montreal being awfully slow at " coming out," I attribute our not absolutely failing on our first appearance. I do not think there was the hire of the room *in,* on the first night ; whereupon, the generous owner so materially reduced the said hire, that albeit disposed to " Up sticks, and off !" after the first attempt, I was induced to try again, and we were rewarded by an eventual bumper. The 17th Regiment was stationed here at the time, and Colonel Gordon gave me the assistance of the band (a very good one), and also his patronage. I shall not easily forget his face, when I asked him for the same, or the puzzled tone of his question, " Are *you* an *actor ?*"*

Well, well ! I had made up my mind to stand anything and every-thing, short of a slap in the face, *in the way of business ;* and, though occasionally my patience was tried, on the whole, I had little to

---

* *Actors* in Canada are a little too much of the Fly-by-night order, to hold a *high* social status.—M. P.

complain of. I here insert a critique on my first appearance in Montreal. that my readers may see the truth of my remark concerning "the agent in advance :"—

"We are happy to say that this novel *soirée musicale* went off, as we predicted, with great *éclát*. The audience certainly did not come up to (in numbers) that we expected, but those who were present had nothing to complain of, and much to praise.   *   *   *   *   * *   *   *   *   *   Miss Lucette's voice is certainly one of the sweetest; her taste is undeniable, and she has evidently been schooled by a first-rate master.*   She gave ' La Brindisi,' from *Traviata*, beautifully.   The Captain is a cool, quiet actor—gentlemanly in his action, and evidently at home at *all points*.   His voice is a high tenor; he takes the great stumbling-block of all tenors, A natural, and even B, with perfect ease from the chest.   The applause was not greater than was deserved by both *artistes*.   A little more publicity would have been of use to both audience and actors.   We trust a second performance may be more generally known to the first, and more remunerative to the second."—*Montreal Herald*.

On the evening of our last performance, a " gentleman" sent to say he wished to see me ; and being in too great a hurry for my supper, to care about an interview with a stranger at the moment, I sent word for him to call the next day at my hotel.   In lieu of doing which, however, he sent me the following note, which, being a gem in its way, I present in its original form :

" Montrall, Toosdy.

" SIR,

" When you recognises this and ther is no cos to be alarmd, becos I have no intenshuns to inshure you.   But if you have the feelins of a gentlman, you will not halow my litel bil to stan aganst you hany longer, and you must have mad a preshus deel lass nite.

" The yung woman as you lef behind took on dredful wen you didn rite, an as gon to New York with a chap as she new afore, so she ant no god.   I never thot as you wood have tuk to hacting, but hops its for the best.

---

* Frank Romer, we thank thee.

" Give the munny to barer, leven shillins and tuppens.   Never mine the apense.

" Your obedent servent,

JAMES ———."

There—the name beat me.   But I think it was Callagher, or Callaghan, or Galloway; but the " barer," when I went to the door to see him, stuttered so awfully, that I could scarcely understand a word he said.   However, Stocks discovered, for me, that some neer-do-weel, rejoicing in the name of " Price," and prefixing the title of " Captain," had some months before victimised the unfortunate James ———, to the tune of " leven shillins and tuppens," for washing ; and as the letter amused me, I give it to you, dear reader, hoping it may have the like effect.

It will be seen by the " bill of fare" of the St. Lawrence Hall, that the English meal, 'yclept supper, is not therein comprehended.   Now, supper to actors and actresses, especially if they are singers, is *the* meal of the twenty-four hours.   Rehearsals are fatal to a good breakfast ; shopping or a nap shuts out lunch ; dinner, no singer will touch.   But supper—dear, delicious, dreamy supper !—there is not a stage votary, from the little tired ballet-girl to the deep-throated tragic star, that doesn't hie him or her home, with happy, or it may be heavy heart, to *supper !*   Supper, he or she must have, or die !   Ergo, in spite of the darkie's discontent and the dreariness of the long since deserted salle-à-manger, supper did we insist upon having ; and our little *tri-angular* party might have been nightly seen any time between eleven and twelve of the clock, in comfortable possession of the far-end corner, cosily employed in their nocturnal orgies.

Our example speedily found backers.   We were one evening engaged as above, when the centre doors opened, apparently in spite of the sable Cerberus' interposition, and a tall lady entered, followed by another and two gentlemen.

" Mon Dieu ! no souper ! I sal faint. Mon cher creature (turning to one of the gentlemen), to make endeavour to procure somting."

GENTLEMAN. " My dear lady, I will speak to the proprietor."

(Exit Gentleman.)

The lady sailed up to our table, and after a searching glance at the viands, her eyes suddenly caught our bottles of *Stout,* and, clapping her hands, joyously, she exclaimed, " Portere Anglaise.   Delicious !"

She was very handsome, and a glance told *us* that she was a professional.   There was the tell-tale darkening under the eye, and the least remnant of enamel on the forehead, of which a hasty toilet had not permitted entire removal.   I whispered Lucille, and the gentleman's returning exclamation, " My dear P——," confirmed our guess.

This was Madame P——, the reigning musical star in the diggings, and every subsequent evening saw Comedy and Opera united in the bond of supper-hood, until time was called, and we separated upon our mutual ways—Parodi and party to New York, I believe ; Lucille, and her "little lot," to Kingston.

However, I am not going to leave Montreal without chronicling the only act *pecuniary* of *hospitality* (my readers must interpret my expressionary peculiarities as they best can) to which I was indebted during my entire tour.   I had become casually acquainted with a gentleman, who from his total lack of likeness in style or conversation to any man I had yet met in Canada, had much interested me.   He was a polished gentleman, a finished sportsman, and a theatrical enthusiast ; by birth, a French Canadian ; by profession——Well, if I name *that,* I may as well give his portrait at once—so we'll pass it, please.

Strangely my liking commenced with a slight *dis*liking, inasmuch as his polite advances, naturally suggested the question, " Is it myself, or *Lucille* he is after ?" However, pleasant drives " round the mountain," and snug rubbers at whist were the only apparent result of this addition to our party, until one evening he announced his departure for somewhere—I forget where ; to some races—I forget what ; and we parted with mutual good wishes.   He intended starting by steamer down the lake, the following morning.

What has this to do with " pecuniary hospitality ?"

Why a great deal, as you will learn.   Go on.

I had been in treaty for a place at Kingston wherein to give our Entertainment, as that city does not boast either of a theatre or a concert-room, and on the morning of our Canadian friend's departure I received a letter desiring me to come *at once,* if we intended coming at all, as the Town Hall was to be had then, and might not by-and-by, *" or words to that effect."*

Annoyingly enough, I had just invested all my superfluous cash in a set of fur robes, and had not left myself " wherewith to make stakes with a street beggar." I had calculated on not leaving Montreal for a week, in which time I knew the needful would be to hand.

A committee of ways and means was called, and one of the council made a sotto-voce suggestion.

" Wouldn't your friend, M——, lend you what you want ?"

" *Your* friend, rather."

" Nonsense ! He said he would be happy to do anything in his power to serve you."

" He did, and looked as if he meant it ; he has not yet left, I should catch him at the depôt ; and here goes, for the first time in my life, to ask an acquaintance, of some three days' standing, to lend me, on my personal appearance, one hundred and fifty dollars. Ha ! ha !—we shall see."

As I anticipated, I caught my friend at the depôt, and with little preliminary made my requirement known to him, concluding thus,— " Do not suppose I shall be the least annoyed, or even disappointed, at your refusing to assist me ; indeed, I am painfully aware of the fact that I am laying myself open to your censure and mistrust. I have no security to offer you other than my word ; no recommendation other than——"

" Your being a gentleman," he interrupted me with ; " in a strange country, in need of a temporary trifling loan. My dear friend, you shall have it." And without further word, he entered the cashier's office, wrote me a cheque for the amount, and, warmly pressing my hand as he gave it me, said, " Write an acknowledgment when you get the cash, and repay me at your earliest convenience. Would that I felt assured of all men's honour as I do yours." His usually mirthful countenance looked serious as he said this, and when I heard, some time afterwards, that a man whom we often saw with him, and whom he styled his " bosom friend," (I forget the blackguard's name), had *let him in* almost to bankruptcy, I saw something very like a prophecy in his last words.

As luck would have it, I might have spared myself the trouble of testing M's. feelings by thus touching his pocket, as I received a remittance from England the following day, just as we were about starting for Kingston ; and having repaid the borrowed money, and duly chronicled the act of " pecuniary hospitality," to Kingston will I now conduct my reader.

"Hi! hi! stop! Why, what the Dickens——," the aforesaid reader will here be shouting. "You Captain—you author, you! Why, you are surely not going away from Montreal without telling us something of the great Victoria Bridge ?"

Well, yes, I was, because the great Victoria Bridge was not finished when I left Montreal, the first time, in August, 1859, but was subjected to my approval as complete in December of that year, when I took my final departure from the city of the descendants of Jacques Cartier ; and as you have asked so bluntly, I will tell you all I know of the Victoria Bridge.

It is considered one of the wonders of the world, and certainly, for size, it is such. I suppose no other building in the creation contains such a mass of stone. I have heard it computed that one buttress of this Goliath is composed of more stuff than there is in all Waterloo Bridge ! I give it to you as I got it, so don't scream at *me*. Well, it— that is, the bridge, not the buttress, (there are five and twenty of them) extends from Point St. Charles, on Montreal side, to some other point on the other side (the south); it is " Tubular," which means you don't go over, but *through* it. It is all but two miles long, and one of the spans is three hundred and thirty feet.

The reason it is made of such prodigious strength is, that it is calculated that at the finish of every winter, when the ice breaks up and comes down the St. Lawrence, the said bridge will have to withstand a pressure of fourteen hundred millions of (I tried to put it in figures, but couldn't) tons of ice ! The Prince of Wales formally gave the concern his blessing last year, and the trains running ever it (through it, I mean), the Grand Trunk Railway can boast of something like 1,200 continuous miles of discomfort from Chicago to Quebec and Portland, the western and eastern termini.

MONTREAL TO KINGSTON.

Wood and water, as before, as always, nothing in the world to enliven the journey, save our own good fellowship, fun, and fancies. The bumping over a portion of this weary journey was truly hurtful; Lucille and I tried to play draughts, but we might as well have tried to play billiards.

The kings lost their crowns, and thereby constantly magnified the common herd; the black subjects kept jumping over the white without any just pretence for so doing; and the whole kingdom became so utterly unruly, that we abandoned the game in despair. Sleeping was a delusion, of course. Oh, be warned my fellow wanderers! *Carry an air-cushion with you.* It is portable as a pocket-handkerchief, or a muffler; and you will find it an immense boon to a weary head.

The carriage, as we progressed, became insufferably hot, and the concomitant dust, unbearable. I have before spoken of the un-eau-de-cologne pervading perfume of these steam propelled 'busses; but I think upon a retrospective analysis of *all* the smells my olfactories had to endure, from time to time, the bouquet on the present occasion was the most powerfully objectionable.

Some more than usually dirty passengers, you suppose.

Well, rather.

On our arrival at Kingston, which we ultimately accomplished, I discovered that for some hours we had been enjoying the privilege of seats, adjoining five or six *convicts* chained together, and reeking in dust and filth, under charge of a constable, bristling with combustibles and beery importance. This, in a first-class carriage!

Some writers have eulogised American politeness towards the "fair sex." During this journey, we had a glaring, but a very amusing instance of *t'other*. Soon after starting, something went wrong with our carriage, and we had all to bundle out, and get in as we best might to another, already three parts full. We, of course, wanted seats together, and our only chance of obtaining such, was in asking a gentleman, who had appropriated *three* for the separate and special comfort of his head, body, legs. His answer to my polite request was as follows :—

" Wa-al, I reckon the lady hain't travelled two hundred everlasting miles—*she* hain't; and nary a wink of sleep the whole of the almighty way! Look at them blessed boots!—they pinch infernal—they do!

They are pretty comfortable jist now—they air ;—and I'd like to see any man, woman, or child, set 'em a goin' again—I would !"

" I thought for a lady——"

" Now, look here, stranger. I guess I've took these seats, and I calculate to keep them until I reach Kington—that's a fact !"

Finding the brute wouldn't move, we accepted the polite invitations of an old French gentleman, who kindly moved a number of his parcels from some otherwise unoccupied seats, and soon made ourselves comfortable thereon.

In about an hour the train came to a halt, and our rude neighbour, whose snoring and grunting had upset Lucille immensely, got up, carefully arranged his horse-cloth and other wraps upon his *seats*, and got out for some purpose or other, giving us, as he did so, an unmistakeable look of defiance. He hadn't been gone one minute, when a huge, hirsute, Californian digger-like individual entered, and, in a twinkling moved said neighbour's entire inventory on to *one* of the seats, plunged himself on to the other two, and had scarcely spat twice when re-enter first ruffian.

FIRST R. (loq.) " Say, stranger, them's my seats !"

SECOND R. " Don't see that, any haow yew fix it !"

FIRST R. " Them's my fixings !" (pointing to articles).

SECOND Do. " Wa-al, I ain't touching 'em."

FIRST R. " But you *have* touched 'em !"

SECOND Do. " That's so ; or haow could I be here ?"

FIRST R. " Well, I guess you had better make tracks out of that, anyway !"

SECOND Do. (with a most expressive grunt) " Look here, stranger. Whar I settles, I settles—that's a fact !" (turning round, and *settling* himself comfortably).

We, of course, enjoyed this immeasurably ; and I completely floored our late enemy by saying, with as good an attempt at Yankee lingo as I was master of, " I guess that's *law*, anyhaow !"

" That's so," said Ruffian No. 2 (bestowing a knowing wink on me). " Two to one agin you, stranger. You'd better clear !"

And No. 1, seeing such was the case, grunted himself into the only spare seat he could find.

This incident I narrate, more because it vastly amused us at the time (and, perchance, what amused us, may amuse you, reader), than to illustrate American lack of manners; for though *I* cannot eulogise their politeness—not having ourselves received any at their hands—I have no reason for thinking them any worse than the mass of the "lords of creation" of any other nation.

We were dreadfully late in arriving at Kingston, and, unfortunately, I had neglected at Montreal to inquire for the best hotel for us to go, to. However, about four A.M. saw us in a "bus," in front of the "British American," vainly endeavouring to obtain an opening. This we at last effected, and, very tired and half famished, we discharged ourselves into a sort of tap-room, and there awaited the arrival from BEDFORDSHIRE of the landlord, who, on his appearance, I greeted with "Landlord, for the love of humanity, give us some beer!"

His cheerful reply, and speedy production of the much-needed beverage, convinced me we had fallen into good hands, and need seek no further. By broad daylight we soon consigned ourselves to our respective couches, for the first time in Kingston.

Kingston!—I have pleasant recollections of Kingston. It has a market-place large enough for ten Kingstons, and—I don't think there is anything else worthy of note in it. The streets seem very wide, some of them *so* wide, that you can't see from one side to the other—but that is because the other is *not yet built*; and, I fancy, never will be. Kingston, I believe, was started in a great hurry, and all sorts of people indulged in all sorts of notions that it was to be the capital of Canada, and they bought land, which they never paid for, and built houses, which they never finished; and if they did, never lived to live in; or if they did, died so soon afterwards, that they had no time to get anyone to inherit them; or if they *had*, the heirs sold the furniture to get whisky, or buy shares in a railway—either of which investment was so profitable that it carried the purchaser off, *right away*, and the house alone remained to tell the tale; and, as it was told me by an old inhabitant "as remembered it long afore there was a house in it"—'twas a melancholy tale, indeed. We paid a *second* visit, however, to Kingston; and when I commit the same to paper, I will tell you more about it. We found a very fine hall, the City Hall, at our service, and secured it for three nights, at the rate of twelve dollars a night. Mr. Barker, the editor and proprietor of " The

British Whig," called on us, and to him we were mainly indebted for the fine audience we obtained on the first evening. He was one of those old gentlemen that young ladies so much like—politeness from his hat to his boots—and Lucille to this day bears the "doctor" in affectionate memory. Doctor! if you ever read this, think of us gently, and know we are not forgetful of your kindness. Well, we achieved great success at Kingston, and there I first sang my now celebrated "Banner of old England," written for me by Mr. Murdoch, late bandmaster of the 71st Light Infantry—then, and I suppose now, musical librarian and leader of the Kingston brass band ("Blow-hards" I christened them), and a thorough good fellow. My new entertainment, as practice made us perfect, was a success, and I had already become so conceited upon it, that the paper was purchased, and the plot prepared for a second production.

There was a detachment of the Canadian Rifles quartered here, and a great many attended our entertainments. One night, after a more than usually enthusiastic encore of my "Banner," I was electrified by hearing a Stentorian voice among the audience exclaim, "Three cheers for Captain *Horton Rhys!*"—when looking to the quarter from whence it proceeded, I discovered as I thought, amid a group of "green coats," a countenance that was familiar to me. This was solved the next morning by the proprietor of said countenance calling on me, and after the usual salute, revealing to me the fact that he "know'd me, as soon as ever he seed me," and "didn't I recollect him as was servant to Captain E——r, when the Cameronians were in China, and was with him when he '*hurt his self*' at Gibraltar?" &c., &c. A great number of my old regiment (the 26th) had exchanged into the Canadian Rifles, on the *hurried* departure of the former regiment, a few years since, from Canada; and this was not the only instance of recognition I encountered on my tour.

We stayed here no longer than our *professional duties* demanded. The town was dull—drearily dull—and a quiet game of billiards, and a row on the lake, the only approach to amusement. However, I learned that in a few weeks' time a "Great Exhibition" was to be held there, and that the town would be "cram full" of all sorts of people, and that I ought to come there then; and, as come there then I did, I'll e'en take my leave of Kingston for the present, and pack up my traps for the next halt on my list,—viz., Cobourg.

CHAPTER VII.

FROM KINGSTON TO COBOURG.

TIRED of the monotony of railway travelling, we determined upon doing this little journey by water, and a very pleasant trip we had. Good steamer, smooth water, and a tolerable table. Cobourg is about half way between Kingston and Toronto ; and I would recommend the traveller on his route to halt here, always taking the precaution to write a day or two previously to the proprietor of the only decent hostelrie in the town, " The Globe," to meet, or send to meet, said traveller, or he will chance to fare as we did on our arrival át eleven o'clock on a wet Thursday night—pitch dark, no lamps, no other passengers, no end of luggage, and no one, and nothing to carry it. I shan't forget it soon.

The indefatigable Stocks was sent out *en scout*, and returned with the semi-melancholy information that they had " found an Hotel, but they had all gone to bed and wouldn't get up, he thought, unless we did ourselves, and we had better leave the luggage, as there was no one wide awake enough to steal it, and come along, at once." And as there was no help for it, " come along" we did ; and after a fierce cannonade at the door, and a parley with one of the windows, we were admitted, and the unfortunate Stocks was sent back to mount guard over the luggage with a bad tooth ache, until an invisible " somebody" arrived with a truck to " bring up" the same, which I believe occurred some time in the morning, for Stocks looked remarkably seedy when he called me, and said he " didn't think much of this here Cobug,"

We had, however, reason for thinking a good deal of it, as we had two capital *rooms*. The concert-hall was in the hotel, and held about four hundred persons, and here I started the plan of having a " Lady and Gentleman's Ticket, 75 cents.," which I always afterwards found to answer. Paterfamilias or affectionate brother didn't hesitate to bring himself at 50 cents., and wife and sister at 25 ; but when he had to fork out a dollar (50 cents apiece) he either stayed away altogether, or " *sneaked himself in, unbeknownst to the females,*" (*vide* Stocks' opinion), " and told 'em afterwards it warn't worth going to see—don't you see ?"

Distant from Cobourg seven miles is a small town, called Port Hope, where, but for the lack of an hotel fit to lay head in, I would also recommend a short sojourn. Anything in the shape of music *does well* there. We gave no less than five entertainments there ; the last, or farewell one, being a " bumper," the room being, according to the " Weekly Guide" of August 30th, "filled with the youth, beauty, fashion, and musical ability of Port Hope."

From Port Hope we journeyed north to Peterborough. This is a portion of my journey that I look back to with much pleasure. I, by this time, began to see my way. My winning the wager was a certainty, bar accidents or ill-health. We were gradually getting into the ways of the country and the habits of the people, and, strangely enough, so it then seemed to us, the farther we got into this strange land, the more Englishified it became ; at least, as far as the inhabitants were concerned.

So, be it understood, I did not go to Peterborough for the purpose of increasing my professional receipts, (though, as luck had it, I did to some extent, most unexpectedly, and as will be seen) ; but rather to investigate a little life amongst the back-woodsmen, and what I saw I will now relate. Peterborough, which is quite a frontier town, there being no other pretension to the term " town" north, or beyond it, is a most eccentric-looking place. Though quite in its infancy, it appears to have grown prematurely aged—a sort of young child with an old man's face.

A few years ago its site was a wilderness. Now there's, I don't know how many but a good lot of people there. Of course, the greater number of the houses, especially the large ones, or those intended to have been large, are, and are likely to remain, in an unfinished state.

The waste of stone in Canada in this respect is wonderful ; everybody commences to build, but nobody ever finishes ; and what is more extraordinary, no one pulls down what any one else puts up. Young Robinson looks with mingled veneration and contempt upon the windowless walls and rafterless roofs of Robinson, senior, long gathered to his ancestors, and says, " Ha, the old man wur a fool to build that 'ere so large, he wur ; *it ain't no use doing anything with* it—not it !" And so it stands until it tumbles down, or Robinson, junior, drinks himself to death, or becomes bankrupt—when possibly an enterprising stranger becomes possessed of the property at the hammer, and something *is* done with it by somebody—not, however, in the time of anybody who saw it built. So is it at Peterborough ; there are whole streets of young ruins.

A gentleman who had a very comfortable house told me, on admiring the loftiness and general arrangement of the rooms, that he was indebted to some one he knew for that, as he had bought the entire shell within which we were then sitting for the price of the materials ; and much to the astonishment of his Canadian neighbours, had floored, roofed, painted and papered the whole concern, without pulling down a brick ; and, he concluded, " It looks pretty sound, too ; don't it ?"

At Peterborough I was destined to meet an old friend with a new face ; he was at Eton with me, and was then and there a very pretty boy ; and being of a retiring mild nature, I had often on more than one occasion taken his part against some juvenile bully. He had come to Canada to *learn farming*, " Heaven save the mark !"—and was *studying* " away out" at a place called Douro, about twelve miles off.

The pretty, retiring, mild youth, had changed into a big-bearded, brawny, bellowing back-woodsman. I never saw such a creature. I told *him* so ; so, of course, I may *you*). If you can fancy Ben Caunt, with an enormous red beard, whiskers, and mustachios, in a Glengarry cap, a red flannel shirt, loose leather breeches, and a pair of knickerbockers, you have (barring the nose) a good likeness of my friend (what shall I call him ?)—" Blazes !"

When he discovered my " little game," as he called it, nothing would satisfy him but that we must and should give our Entertainment in Peterborough. " He would bring in all his friends from Douro, he would keep them and himself perfectly sober until it was all over ; and if everybody in Peterborough didn't come, he'd know the reason why !" &c., &c., &c. To such powerful arguments we could but succumb, and, much to our surprise, we discovered that there was a little amateur theatre in the town, called " White's Room." At this time I had just written a new entertainment, called *A Scene in the Highlands,* and being anxious for a rehearsal, and having little dread of Peterborough critics, we " concluded" to play, and did so, with such success, and to such crowded and respectable audiences (whether owing to our friend *Blazes'* persuasion or threats I know not), that not content with *two* nights, we played four ! I thought Lucille's hearers would never be satisfied with " Ever of thee," " Annie Laurie," and " I'm sitting by the stile; Mary." They *would* have her back, time after time ; and I think if *I* had been exiled there, I should have done the same. *Blazes* persisted in *crying* over " I'm sitting by the stile, Mary," and said he was an Irishman, though I know he used to be a Londoner. This, however, was late in the evening.

Having thus paid our way, and a little to spare, I determined on a slight relaxation from mental labour, and ditto a little in the body. Douro, I have said, is a " diggings" some twelve miles from Peterborough, and is a regular stronghold of sucking farmers. Suckers, and no mistake ! Their powers of suction would astonish a Pitman !

Well, this Douro is right in the bush, and if any of my readers *should* journey from Peterborough to Douro, they'll wonder how it ever got there ; a more villanous road I never travelled, though my friend *Blazes* (of course), and also *his* friend (another long, but not *so* rough-looking customer, who had something to do with the lumber—i.e. timber trade), declared " 'twas nuts to what it *was !*"

I was glad that a slight cold prevented Lucille from being one of the party, though that fact prevented me from staying to see and do all that I should have wished. A deer hunt, of course, we had—that is to say, the dogs had, and having, I suppose, " By raison of being a sthranger," as a *boná fide* Irishman of the party said, been put in a " convaynient" position—which meant that I could neither see or be seen—and told to keep my eyes and ears open, and my mouth shut, I had my first and last acquaintance with a Canadian Deer Hunt.

I think I must have been two hours in this *convaynient* spot, listening to the cry of the hounds. Oh ! yes, *they were* hounds !—all sorts ; but that didn't signify. Sometimes quite near, then away in the forest—all still ! The birds had been scared, and were quiet—then, swelling louder and louder, and sounds of crashing boughs and the quick slobbering breath of a hound, as, with bloody stern and fiery eye, he passed, within a yard of me—slightly at fault. I deuced nearly shot him, he startled

me so; and all is still again. If I had known my way, I should then
and there have walked myself off; but I didn't, so couldn't.

For some time past I had kept my eye on a green patch of sward, or
stagnant water, I couldn't tell which; distant off, guessed some one
hundred and fifty yards. This was only visible through a very narrow
opening in the wood; and a few minutes after the episode of the hound,
I again cast my eye towards it. I could no longer see it! Holloa!
I thought, I have been straining my eyes a leetle too much; and I
moved suddenly, when as suddenly something else moved, and I saw the
green patch, and I saw a brown patch, and I sent a *dis*patch after brown
patch, just as it was jumping over green; and then ran like a madman
down the opening to see what on earth I had done! Done, sir? Why,
I had done for a fine deer, by sending a bullet from the right-hand
barrel of my little " Laing's" rifle, slick through his body, behind the
shoulder!—and a good shot it was, too, with such a " pop-gun," as
Blazes termed it.

" The shades of night were fast falling" (there's a bit of *novelism* for
you) when we got home—I mean when we returned to Douro, the
Canadian home of my friend *Blazes*. Let me see,—what was it he
termed it ? Oh, his " Penal Penates !" I think I never saw a *wetter*
evening; the elements—i.e. whisky, rum, gin and water—were irre-
sistible in their unceasing flow. So, if my journal here becomes a little
foggy, pray pardon me, and allow me to " *turn in*," for the first time
since my departure from England, under other roof than that which
sheltered my compagnons du voyage.

*   *   *   *   *   *

Breakfast at seven. " Any head-ache ?" " No ?" "What do you
say to fishing ?"

" Why, you know," I said, " *that* was what I came here for."

" *And* the whisky ?"

" Bother the whisky !"

" Well, you *were* ' tight ;' and I shall tell your friends that I took
care of you."

The speaker was so utterly "sewn up" some two hours before the
party quite dispersed, that he slept where he fell, and never " turned in"
at all.

Fishing, some two or three of us went; and if I at all astonished these rough sons of Englishmen with my "pop-gun," I did so still more with my rod. It was an ordinary trout rod, made by an old fellow named Hucklebridge, in Bath, (one that I have fished with over fifteen years), and with a few sewin flies (my friends used bait), I succeeded in landing, or rather in *boat*ing, for I fished principally from the latter, thirteen bass—a fish neither a salmon, a trout, nor a grayling, but (with a dash of the porpoise) a little of all combined. They averaged three pounds apiece. But, bless you! a good old English trout of that weight would have made my ancient piece of hickory bend its back a little more that any of them did.

They were, however, good fun. There was a nice breeze, and the *thing was new*; and that goes a long way towards temporary satisfaction.

Blazes was a great hand at a canoe, and after I was tired of fishing, he insisted on paddling me up a lake, I forget the name, where he said he had appointed to meet an Indian.

" What—a real live Indian ?"

" I believe you, my bo-hoy !"

Now, I had often wished to see an Indian, and, like most things that one wishes much to see, when I *did* see one, I didn't think much of it.

The dark and almost indecent individual we were in quest of, made a sudden appearance in answer to an unearthly screech from the lungs of my Charon, as we neared the shore of a thickly-wooded eyot. Paddling over the tiny waves with a marvellous rapidity in a similar unsafe looking concern to that we were in, he came alongside ; and after an interchange with Blazes of a few words in French and Chinese—at least it sounded like it—and an awful lot of grimaces, he pointed at me with the spoon end of his paddle, saying, or rather shouting, " Hi-phiz, cockonoscrummery !" or *words to that effect*, and darted off ; and, much to my surprise, we after him !

" Where are you going to ?" I asked.

" Going ! Going to introduce you to my father-in-law, that is to be !" he answered, paddling away with all his might.

" Your what ?"

" Yes ; it's all right ! That's my wife's brother, on ahead, there !"

" Get out !" I exclaimed, forgetting I was in a canoe, and bestowing a kick on his shins.

"By. G—d !" was his reply, " we shall both *get out* sooner than we can get in again, if you come any of those games. Sit still, man !—you are not in bed !"

Thus admonished, I collapsed.

We shortly reached a large raft moored along-side a steep bank, the bank itself being nearly hidden from view by overhanging trees and bush. Blazes here pulled up, and told *me* (this time) to " Get out !"—a performance of no easy accomplishment. Canoes are the most slippery things in creation—our outriggers are jolly-boats to them. Out, however, I got, after a deal of wibble-wobbling ; and Blazes paddled off somewhere out of sight, much to my momentary discomfiture. He, however, quickly appeared on the bank overhead, and from thence directed me to a flight of steps, or rather stones, which I had not until then perceived. I ascended, and found myself on a little green knoll, with large tree stumps here and there, and studded around with huts apparently made of logs and bark of trees. Well, I never!—I was actually in an Indian encampment ! There were men and women, and children and dogs ; and Blazes seemed on intimate terms with all.

He presently introduced me to a venerable-looking old picture card, wrapped—although it was very hot—in a buffalo skin, and squatted on his haunches smoking a red clay pipe, with a profusely ornamented stem.

" Father-in-law," he said, " this is my friend—a mighty hunter in England—a great warrior in many lands — and a jolly good fellow !"

This correct description, being given in English, not a word, of course, the old gentleman would have understood, but for the expressive pantomime with which it was accompanied. It, however, evidently impressed the aged Ojibbeway that I was somebody ; and he thereupon set up a howl of welcome, and beckoned me to squat. This, imagining myself tolerably secure, I did, and looked about me ; and thereupon saw the retreating form of Blazes on the point of entering one of the huts. Now, I had no intention of being left alone with this old heathen, so I *made tracks* after him, and affectionately taking his arm, I requested

Blazes to bear the same in mind. He looked annoyed—which, how-ever, did not affect me in the least, and we entered together.

There were only two occupants—a frightfully plain specimen of an aged female, *and* a girl of about fifteen or sixteen. They were both employed in embroidering velvet with beads. Immediately the younger of the two saw my companion, she sprang up, and jumped into his arms, and in (as far as I am a judge) very fair French, welcomed him, said she had been expecting his visit; and it was evidently a lover's meeting. I *must* describe her. She had very little on; what she had, appearing to me to be a blue serge petticoat, with some sort of embroidery round the skirt, over which was a dingy white " *cutty sark*," confined at the waist with a beadwork embroidered girdle, and over this, a man's work-a-day cloth jacket, with large mother-o'-pearl buttons! Her hair was jet black, with a sort of oily look about it I didn't quite like; but, lor! she had enough for a dozen women—I never saw such a magnificent mop! If she had put it *à l'Anglaise* into a net at the back of her head, she would never have seen her toes again! Her complexion was brown—yes, *brown*—the brown of the ripe filbert. Her nose was perfect, if not *too* small;—her mouth a little large. But—murder! such red lips and white teeth, you almost wished it larger, that the vermillion and the pearl might show the more;—and her eyes—well, *there* I am beaten. Suffice it to say, that I never saw such eyes for black ones. I dreamt of them more than once afterwards. Her head was beautifully put on; and her legs, which were naked to the knee, were the *moral* of Louise Leclercq's brown silk stockings. I never *could* see any beauty in a naked foot—especially when the sole was as hard as nails—so, I'll leave her *foot* alone—excepting to say, it looked very small.

But I am over-spinning my yarn. These were the wife and grand-daughter of the old gentleman whose society I had so rudely declined. Blazes was desperately in love with the girl; it seems he had some months previously picked her out of the water as she was vainly endeavouring to right her canoe, which had topsy turvied. They swim like corks (the women, I mean); but she was nearly exhausted with her efforts, being very young; and would most likely have been drowned, but for *Blazes'* assistance. Of course, the old ones were immensely grateful for the preservation of their " che-ild;" and would have tattoed, or otherwise ennobled Blazes upon the spot, had he wished it. But he didn't : he made himself, however, a sort of godfather to the young Naiad, and had succeeded in teaching her French and a smattering of English ; and I think he said she could write " a tolerable fist."

We stayed until our watches warned us to be off—for darkness in Canada, like the thunder-storm, comes on you, *bang*—without the prelude of twilight ; and I didn't care much about remaining after night-fall in this wild region, even under the wing of *Blazes*. Had there been a twin Naiad I might have been reconciled ; but there wasn't.

I shall ever remember our homeward voyage, through the beauty of that night. Squatted in the stern of the canoe, with a delicious pipe of tobacco in my mouth, I watched the deep shadows of the bush-covered shore as the moon rose—full, large, and red—lighting up the waters, but throwing land and forest into deeper gloom. My companion paddled leisurely along, playing, as it were, with the sparkling water ; and our little bark went bobbity-bobbity, as much as to say, " I should just like to pitch you two out, you seem so jolly lazy !"

Blazes was evidently buried in a *brown* study, and I didn't care much about interrupting him. I, too, was tkinking—thinking of a picture I had somewhere seen of a very dark girl and a very fair one ;—and wishing that I were an artist, that I might put on canvas the darkest and the fairest beauty in creation. Heigho !

Nothing occurred to disturb the even tenur of our way ; and on we went, paddling and puffing—an occasional snatch of a song on my part, and a melancholy effort at a second on his, alone mingling with the gurgling of the water at the bow of the canoe and the hum of many insects in the air. We arrived at the landing-stage, and there found a servant waiting with a trap, and, what much gladdened my eyes, a bottle of whisky, for we long since had finished the flask that accompanied us. We had only a few miles to go to " *Blazes' Park*"—as I termed his few acres of clearing—and whether it was the whisky or jolting, I know not, but Blazes at last opened his mouth, and blurted out, " I say, old fellow, I'm going to marry that nigger lass !"

" *Marry ?*" I said, putting the bowl end of my pipe in my astonishment
to my lips—" the devil !"

" Nearly as black, certainly," he replied, mistaking my exclamation ;
" but there's more of the angel in her than the devil—anyhow !"

" My dear man, I didn't mean that——"

" No, no ; I know. Of course, you'll laugh ; but mark my words :
if you ever come to Douro again, you'll find that girl in my house—my
lawful wife !"

He made his words good ; for in spite of the jeers of his wild band
of companions, he carried her off one fine night, and *married* her by
book and candle (Blazes is a Roman Catholic) ; and, as he is next heir
to many a broad acre in " Merrie England," it is just possible I may
yet again see the heroine of this little yarn, and presiding over a very
different establishment to that in her Indian home.

We must bid adieu to Douro and Peterborough (I have made too long
a halt here already), and will ask my reader to come with me to Toronto,
which was our next quarters—though we did not long occupy them, in
consequence of what is told in the next Chapter.

CHAPTER VIII.

To get to Toronto we had to retrace our steps to Port Hope, that we might "catch the train"—the Grand Trunk Railway of Canada passing through those places ;—and though warm as had been our welcome at the latter town, I left it without sorrow, the hotel accommodation being the worst we had yet met with.   Indeed, the rapacity and chicanery displayed by the proprietor of the British American Hotel in that place in the manufacture of his bill, was something too glaring to be passed over in silence.   Had I *had* the time I would have disputed his claim, and, indeed, saw a lawyer on the matter; but Master "Paddy" (the shark was an Irishman) knew I *hadn't*, and pocketed his ill-earned dollars in safety.

Toronto is the capital of Canada West ; and I have either read or been told that less than sixty years ago *two* native families were its only inhabitants—barring the beasts and birds.   In some five and twenty years they had increased (*not* the beasts and birds, there was no census taken of *them*) to 1,400 items ; and now (including myself and party) amount to 60,000.   There must be something in the air, HERE !

Toronto is the handsomest town we have yet seen.   Wide streets, good shops, lovely gardens, handsome public buildings, churches rich in spires and traceried windows, spacious hotels, and elegant equipages. We put up at the Revere House, and during our stay, there was a grand Scottish gathering.   Such piping and dancing, and throwing the caber ! Glorious weather, bands playing, handsome women, wonderful calves (the men, I mean—that is, the men's legs) ; and yet, we only stayed two days.   Business, my dear sir—business !   We had no *business* there, happening this wise.

On leaving Kingston, my good friend, Dr. Barker, gave me a letter of introduction to *the Honorable Mr. Brown, the Editor and Proprietor of* "The Globe" *newspaper*, which I forwarded, with an order to do me certain posters, bills, &c., and a request that he would give me a few lines in his paper of preliminary notice. My *request* the honorable Brown complied with ; but the *order* was entirely neglected. *Nary a* bill, a poster, or even advertisement were done, or in process of doing, when we arrived. Of course, my first visit was to the office of " The Globe ;" and it is quite possible that when I arrived thereat, I might not have been in the best of humours, for on my way thither I passed some tremendous *hoardings,* profusely decorated with every sort of advertisement, *sine* mine. I had stopped at a reading-room, and read the advertising columns of all the Toronto papers, " Globe" included—mine was invisible. I had met a friend whose acquaintance I had made at Quebec—a lawyer, a banker, and a most influential member of Toronto society, and he asked me, " If I meant to give my Entertainment there ?" Well, I was *not* in a good humour ; and, after some five minutes conversation in the " Globe" office, with a hungry-looking, bald-headed individual, in his shirt-sleeves, and nails in mourning, I desired to see the Honorable Brown himself. Much to my surprise, I found that he stood before me.

In reply to my reiterated question, " Why the order was not completed ?" he replied, " That owing to the printers in general being constantly *done* by the travelling profession (murder !) that they had determined on giving no more credit."

I inquired if a letter of introduction and recommendation from a brother editor " went for nothing."

He suddenly remembered he had forgotten that, and was thereupon a shade more liberal—offering to do what was required immediately, upon receiving twelve dollars in advance. Whereupon, this child's dander being considerably aroused, I requested the Honorable Brown not to trouble himself, as experience had taught me that Canadian newspaper editors were still less to be trusted than even the " travelling profession."

The Honorable Brown (by-the-bye, reader, in your ig——I mean— innocence, you will wonder what the editor of the " Globe" was doing with, or had done, to get *Honorable* tacked to his name). Good gracious ! sir and madam, he was a member of Parliament, a representative of the people, a stump orator—a very great man, I assure you ; and the

members of the Canadian Parliament having one day, in the exuberance
of their humility, conferred on themselves the title of honorable, *nem.
dis.* so did John Brown become honorable.

Well, Hon. B., expressed much disgust at my style of conversation,
and we parted with mutual *satisfaction.* Well—I don't include Brown in
this " we"—subsequently played one night at Toronto, but we did not in
any way increase the Honorable Brown's exchequer, as we employed his
adversary, " The Leader"—a paper of nearly equal circulation, and
infinitely better type.

We had not a very large audience, and the papers, in their critiques,
were flattering enough : even the " Globe" gave us κυδος, com-
plained of the lack of publicity given, and suggested another Evening's
Entertainment. I, however, didn't care much about Toronto; there
was too much assumption of exclusiveness, without just grounds *to go
upon,* and I left the place then, as I do now, without any intention of
returning to it.

———————

From Toronto, we shaped our course, south and west, to Hamilton—a
town situated on the extreme west of Lake Ontario. Now, I have a
great deal to say about Hamilton; so, reader, bear with me awhile, or
skip the whole concern to see what comes next ; and when you are *very*
hard up for a ten minutes' pastime, turn back again.

Some of my pleasantest hours in Canada I spent in Hamilton.
Firstly, the hotel in which we were located, " The Royal," was one of
the best we had yet enclosed ourselves in. Dr. Taylor, the proprietor,
is an ancient Englishman of great varied experience, an amusing companion, and liberal host ; a *"smart"* man, too, yet occasionally, like
most smart men, over-reached by a *smarterer.* Eh, Doctor? Shall I
tell, or not ? I am open to a bribe of secrecy, and will wait to hear
how you are disposed, before I promulgate how a certain Loafer
sojourned at the Royal (pray don't think me the Loafer, reader !)—*how*
the Doctor advanced the Loafer five hundred dols., and *how* the Doctor
never saw said Loafer again, and all about it. *Nary* another word,
Doctor, for the present. Move on.

Our stay at Hamilton, was marked with signal success in a professional light.   We gave five sucessive entertainments there, and did well.   We played at the Mechanics' Hall—a fine one for singing in ;—well situated, and tolerably cheap—15 dols. a night ; but they have an ugly custom of charging 2 dols. a week for a licence, which, small as the sum is, being a " do," enrages one, as you are not told of it at the time ; and if you open on the Saturday night and play on the following Monday, as was my case, you are taxed as if you had played two weeks.   This I kicked up such a row about, that perchance my successors may find the imposition removed ; I hope so.   At all events, I have herein warned them.

We played also at the Templars' Hall, a charming little room well worthy of a trial by any one attempting Entertainments.   Not so well situated as the Mechanics', but not *half the price* ; and people will go there as readily as to the other, if the entertainment be *worthy* of a visit.

Hamilton is curiously inhabited.   There are more Englishmen there without any apparent occupation, and living upon apparently nothing, than in any other town *in* Canada.   There are lots of billiard tables, and they (the inhabitants) play ;—there is a cricket ground—but I never saw any of *them* there, except in the capacity of lookers on.   They seem to be an exiled lot, always looking out for, and expecting something that never turns up. They are constantly in the various stores—i.e. shops— which here are good, without display, but never seem to purchase any-thing ; and, in short, I never could make head or tail of them.

Germans, too, here abound.   *They* are principally dealers in Lager bier and professors of music—many of them combining the two pro-fessions—finding, I fancy, the former unprofitable without the latter, and the latter *dry* without the former.

One of these professors played for us three nights, and on each occasion made a dreadful "mull" of it.   I thought he was nervously excited, but was afterwards informed that he was exceedingly drunk, and in sending for his bill found that he expected to get three dols. a night for half an hour's work.   I paid him *two*, and had the gratifica-tion of seeing him, a few nights afterwards, playing on an old stringed instrument in an underground Lager bier establishment, for his supper, and a limited allowance of the delectable liquid. Beware of German professors !

After a very pleasant stay of three or four weeks at Hamilton, we returned, as we had pre-arranged to do, to Kingston, for the " Great Exhibition" week ; and, according to promise, I will now tell you a little more about Kingston than I did before.

There are but two hotels in Kingston where a body may comfortably roost—" The British American," and " Irons' Hotel." I believe the latter *is* called an *hotel*. The former we put up at, and a most comfortable house it is. Mr. Kent, the landlord, and his pretty sister, are the best caterers in every respect ; so, of course, I say to my followers, go thither ! However, on the present occasion, as the sitting room we on our former visit occupied was metamorphosed into a bed-room, or room of beds, for I believe they pigged about a dozen in it, nightly, we went to a little cottage on the outskirts of the town, kept by a Mrs. Green, by which we saved innumerable dollars, and lost a deal of inconvenience from the crowd, dust, noise, &c. To anyone going to Kingston, and preferring a lodging to an inn, I can recommend Mrs. Green and her unpretending, but scrupulously clean cottage. It is well known ; so, easily found.

The public buildings of Kingston are ridiculously large for the requirements of the place ; they are, moreover, handsome ;—but there is nothing in them, and they stand alone in melancholy magnificence. The shops go in couples—two music stores, two drapers, two printers ;—two everything, side by side in inert rivalry. They all are fast closed at seven o'clock, as are the eyes of their proprietors at eight ; and the lamps when they *are* lighted, go out simultaneously with the cats—who, by-the-way, are the most rampaginous crew I ever had the misfortune to *listen* to.

The inhabitants seem principally Irish and Scotch, and are very dirty and discontented, and most prolific (I speak of the lower orders). One young lady was presented to us upon her safe delivery of *four* fine boys ; and I was told the same good luck had attended no less than three *industrious* families during the present year. Great Nature! I fancy the Kingstonites must have had something to do with the before-mentioned rapid populating of Toronto. But it is not a matter of history, or any matter of mine—so, *en resume.*

On sallying forth on the morning after our arrival, and a lovely morning it was, the strangest of all strange crowds thronged the streets. Every manner of man, from the cloaked Indian or rough back-woodsman, up to the French Canadian swell or sombre-coated officer of Canadian Rifles; and women!—all attempt at describing *them* would fall far short of fact. I do think I saw some of the loveliest specimens of " Earth's fairest daughters," in an unpolished state, my eyes ever looked on. I saw, seated on the front seat of a rudely constructed waggon, one young girl, not more than seventeen I should say, slight, but round as an apple stem, who finding the sun warmish to her naked shoulders, let her hair down, tuck it in *under her*, as if it were a garment, and then slily make a loop-hole in her tresses, through which to keep up the fire of her eyes upon the countenance of her swarthy male companion, apparently the most ardent of lovers.

There were, also, as the day waxed older, no end of "fine ladies,' but *they* are the same everywhere; and, as I don't think they excel either in beauty or style in Canada, " least said, soonest mended !"

Vehicles of every description, and beyond all description; so, it is no use my trying at——. The Exhibition itself took place in, or rather the place that took in the Exhibition, was a large glass case about a mile out of the town; and the Exhibition comprised, and the case contained everything inanimate, from a sheet anchor to a shirt-pin. All, *I* thought, of an inferior or antediluvian description. The furs, skins, horns, tusks, and stuffed animal and bird specimens, much excited me, and extracted a great deal of superfluous cash from my pocket. Beyond these, I was not tempted.

There was a Cattle Show; but—shades of my ancestral short-horns! *they* fell very short of every animal useful, or eatable essential.

Lucille roared at the pigs, and ran away from the cows—which were decidedly of the genus wild ;—and, I should opine, wicked to boot.

Evening came, and with it our first performance at "The Sons of Temperance" Hall. (There's a name for you !) The City Hall was engaged by the Exhibition judges, &c. It was not a large room, and our stage was a joke, as a shake hands therefromwith all the reserved seats was quite practicable. That, however, didn't matter ; and people came in crowds, and sat on each other's laps, and cracked nuts, and ate apples, and paid their dollar a head like sensible holiday people, as they were.

This went on every night throughout the week, until Saturday, when a most awful reverse occurred—unequalled, unparalleled—un— Good gracious !

At the usual time on this eventful evening we repaired to the hall, fully calculating on completing the sum of 500 dollars (receipts of five nights, we should then have played), being only fifty dollars short of that amount; and in high glee, we undressed, and were three parts dressed, when it suddenly struck me that the assembling (as I supposed) audience were unusually orderly, and I communicated my opinion through our curtain-screen to Lucille, who replied, " That she supposed that they had drank up all their money, and were sober."

Our faithful slavey at this juncture made his appearance, his serio-comic mug manifesting considerable uneasiness. He volunteered his opinion as follows :—

" Please, sir, I somehow think there won't be no one here to night."

" What ?"

" No one are comed yet"

" Eh ?"

" Only the two gals from the house—free—as is sitting in front seats."

" Bless my soul !"

" Yes, sir."

" Oh, they'll tumble in by-and-bye, I dare say."

" Then they must tumble out a-bed, a purpose."

" Bed !"

" Yes, sir, all gone long ago—town quite empty—Exhibition shut up, and all the shutters, and nobody anywheres."

" Then we had better shut up, too, I suppose ?"

" Yes sir ; and send sharp for the beer at supper, or you won't get none, 'cos all the bar people's done up, and they won't wake up for nobody—'cos I tried as I come along, and there's a gentleman down stairs wants to see you."

*   *   *   *   *   *   *

The first burst of disgust over, we laughed immensely over our blighted hopes, and Lucille asked me, " Why our room was like the Port wine, that day, at luncheon ?"

" Because there was no(*body*) in it."

Anything was better than being serious—so, my dear, yet I fear me outraged, reader, you must guess *how* jolly we were by the fact that I forgave Lucille *the joke*.

We found upon investigation that everybody *had* gone to bed, and even the cats were scarce and comparatively quiet ; not a soul came to the Hall but " the gentleman down stairs," who had driven twelve miles to see us play, and of course didn't.   He declared it was three years since he had taken the trouble of " hossing" it into Kingston, and this would be his last visit in the flesh.   He swore a little, and left ; his retiring audible words being, " Al-*ways* said as this Kings*town* was the d——st hole out west, and now I knows it !   Ga way, hoss !"

I beg to say that our audiences during the Exhibition week were of a totally different order to those who attended our former entertainments, and do so that my kind friends at Kingston, should any of them read these pages, may not think I class *them* with our nut-cracking, apple-munching patrons of the present, or rather just past occasion.

" A little circumstance" which annoyed me at the time, I must here mention, with the philanthropic hope of preventing anyone else from being similarly annoyed.

I had received a letter from my agent in England, with a draft upon the Bank of British North America, drawn by one of their own English branches.   This I presented at the office of the Kingston Branch of the said bank, when *they* told me I must take or send it to New York—'twas of no use anywhere else.   I asked them to telegraph to New York at my expense, to ask if it was there advised, and was told by the head man—and a very rude head man, toc—that they did not act upon telegraph messages, or attend in any way to them.

So, if I had been "hard up" I should have had to have kicked my heels amongst the Kingstonites and the cats, for some four or five days before I could have obtained the money, which then would have been subjected to *black mail* in the shape of " collecting." The branch from the main bank, forsooth ! Moral :—When you travel in Canada, have a letter of credit on a Canadian bank, or the cash in Canadian notes, for you will get neither civility nor assistance from those who, in the same position in England, are ever willing to give both, and even strain a point to oblige a *bonà fide* and accredited traveller.

At Montreal, on one occasion, I had a £100 Bank of England Post Bill going the rounds of the banks for two days, the reason generally assigned for the refusal of *negotiating*, being "that they had more English paper than they wanted." But at no bank did I receive downright incivility, but at the branch bank of the Bank of British North America, in Kingston. I promised the gentleman behind the counter I would remember him, and having done so, hie we on with our "discourse."

On the day following the lamentable termination of our Kingston performances, two gentlemen called and asked me what I would take to go to Belleville, a small town some forty miles north west of Kingston, and play two nights.

Having an object in view—viz., to complete a certain sum of money by a certain time, and also having a vague idea that I might be shortly called upon to disburse more than I was likely to make (for which when found make note of), I agreed to give two entertainments at the theatre, which was represented to me as new, just finished, and a perfect bijou, for 50 dols. each night ; and, the bargain closed, off we started for Belleville.

CHAPTER IX.

BELLEVILLE.

OF all the melancholy, miserable, misanthropic-looking places I ever saw, Belleville is the beau ideal. It " *beats Banagher.*" About a year back, a large portion was burnt down, and the blackened ruins still stand, and seem likely to stand, unless the wind blows them down, which is also likely; in either case I am sure there would be no attempt to rebuild them. There are two banks, but I don't think there's any money in them, for they are situated quite unsafely some way out of the town. There is one hotel, and therein was our only solace. The *Defoe House*, kept by Mr. Warren, is a most comfortable hostelrie, and reasonable in charges. The theatre in which we played *was* new with a vengeance—*so* new that it consisted of simply lath and plaster; the lessee, a Mr. Lester, did all he could to make it endurable, but—ye gods! I never *was* so cold, and Lucille and myself to this day regret having taken fifty dols. a night to play at Belleville. The audience, numerous and respectable on the first night, would not turn out on the second; but having signified their approval of the performance by a deputation from some of the " leading inhabitants," and Mr. Warren having kindly offered the free use of his large dining-room, we played a third night, on our own account, to a *paying* audience, who were kind enough to forgive our involuntary variations in the shape of sneezings, wheezings, and other unmusical introductions. The press (that is, the one paper) was lenient, and our bill was light, so, *malgré* the exceeding dulness of the town, we left Belleville with a blessing. Ho! back to Hamilton.

What did we go back to Hamilton for?

Why, because everybody was going to Hamilton, of course, to see the great Cricket Match between the All England Eleven and the Canadian Twenty-two, and which *I* was not not going to miss, if I knew it; I couldn't get away to see the game either at Montreal or New York, which I shall always regret, that at the latter place especially, as I should not only have considerable benefited my banker's account, but should have had the consummate gratification of *seeing* the self-supposed invincible New York Twenty-two and their backers, taken down an infinity of pegs—a result which I publicly prophesied when and wherever I had an opportunity of so doing, during my late sojourn in New York. As it was, however, I *did* manage to relieve one Republican enthusiast of his odds of four to one, to the tune of eight hundred dollars.

We arrived at our old quarters, in Hamilton, on the same day (Sunday, October 16th), as did Mr. Pickering, the factotum and commander-in-chief of the British Forces, albeit fighting on the other side. This may read strangely to many, through the cricket-playing portion of my readers will easily understand me, so—" Nuff said."

This gentleman I remembered being at Eton with me so forthwith introduced myself to his notice, and found him, as I have all Etonians, at home or abroad, a right good fellow. What Etonian of—well, a certain age, does not recollect " B—l" Pickering? Cannot I now see him seconding Boudier, in his memorable tournay with black Tom, the fighting chimney-sweep, in Batchelor's Acre, or heading the score in Upper Shooting Fields, with no covering to his head but Nature's thatch (which, habit, by-the-bye, he still sticks to*). However, go ahead ; I've no time much to individualize.

The whole town and neighbourhood were on the *qui vive* early in the morning of Monday, to see the all-conquering cricket champions, and Hamilton looked positively excited.

The Eleven put up at the opposition house, " The Anglo-American," the proprietor of that establishment having volunteered to *lodge* them for nothing. Opposition for ever.

The doctor's face was fine when he heard of his rival's liberality.

" Ha! ha! they'll find out what *nothing* means, before they go, I'll warrant;" and I believe they *did*, But, as I understand my good friend J. Lillywhite, is publishing the Tour of the Cricketers, I shall leave him

---

* No pun intended.

to state his reminiscences on that *score,* and proceed with my own. I was, of course, personally known to many of the Eleven, and much bothered they seemed to be at my change of name and appearance, and " Why, captain, what have you done with your whiskers ?" was a question, like the Yankee, " What do you think of the country ?" I got tired of answering.

The first day's play did not commence until late in the afternoon, but I went to the ground, and soon saw enough to assure me that my little odds (of course, on the professionals), were safe, and that the Eleven were not going to lose any laurels *there.* On the second day, Lucille, of course, must go, and notwithstanding she was furred to the eyes, the cold was so intense, that, having *our* own game in view, we soon quitted one of the largest cricket *audiences* I ever saw. The numbers were computed at eleven thousand. I thought there were more.

The Eleven turned out in the evening to see our entertainment, and, of course, more than shared the honours thereof. That we didn't mind, as they had no share in the " gate money," which on that evening was remunerative. The following day, the third and last of the match, the weather was of such an anti-cricket description, and so unmercifully cold, that there was not a third of the former days' attendance ; but those who did go, had such an eye-opener in Caffyn and Jackson (I think) who went in and scored the required number to win, forty-two, without giving a chance to the shivering twenty-two Fielders, that I do not think the Hamiltonians will care again to subscribe to such another three days' farce.

It is a fact, though, perhaps, a hitherto-unrecorded one, that on the day just mentioned, the Eleven having to go in, as before stated, for forty-two to win, so sure were they of doing it, that *two* of *them* only went to the ground ; and the assertion laughed at over night, of, " If it isn't finer to-morrow, there will be only *two* of *us* wanted," was verified to the very letter—*they,* Jackson and Caffyn, *made the required score, and carried out their bats,* Caffyn playing the greater part of the time in his great-coat!

And now, Hamilton, I have to be ashamed of you—you, aspiring city, and would be Queen of the West—with more Englishmen re-

siding in your limits than any other town in Canada—you, because
(it could scarcely be for any other reason) your dearly beloved Canadian Twenty-two were beaten at a game they considered themselves equal
if not superior to any Englishmen that could be " brought all that
way" (eh . my dear B ?) to play them. You refuse in council to
give this unrivalled team the complimentary dinner, vouchsafed to
them by Americans and Canadians on all their other battle-grounds !

In sheer disgust at this unexpected shabbiness, I—yes, *I*, Oh, reader—
sent an invitation to the Eleven, umpires, and followers, to dine
with me at " The Royal," which, however, Mr. Pickering declined,
upon the ground of having to start at seven o'clock the next morning
for Rochester, though what *that* had to do with dining at six the
night before, I don't know. I suppose Mr. P. did. Eheu ! Time
was, when he didn't.

A few words more about that Eleven, and I have done. I don't
think their cricketing friends in England have half appreciated the
adventure. They would, if they only knew the temptations to which
those eleven men were subjected in the course of their tour, and it
redounds immensely to their credit, one and all, that they should
have passed through the ordeal in the manly, upright manner in which,
like thoroughbred cricketers, they did. The Americans, especially
New Yorkers, were greatly annoyed at their keeping themselves so
much to themselves—i.e. not visiting the innumerable restaurants
and other haunts of the thirsty, and poisoning their " innards" with the
various vile concoctions, 'yclept " cocktails," " smashes," " egg nogs,"
&c., &c., therein dispensed.

Somebody speaking to me of their abstemiousness from spirits, said,
" I guess champagne must be cheaper in your country than in ourn,
those cricket chaps did nothing but drink it all day long ; kinder expensive keeping, I reckon. Say, how much do they airn a day, now?"

On my expressing my inability to say, he " *conclewded*" that " them
darned democratic drinks kinder disagreed with their cussed proud
stomicks. Set of darned shoe-makers, and sorter servants. Yah !"

I could mention many amusing anecdotes connected with the celebrated visit of the All England Eleven ; but Mr. L. and his book hang

over my head like the fabled sword—so, I shall selfishly preserve them for my own drawing-room, or rather dining-room Entertainment, and leave Mr. L. to bestow them on the public.

I now approach a subject on which I shall, of course, be expected to dilate to the full stretch of my powers, both of poetry and prose.

*   *   *   *   *

No, sir, and madam, can't do it. I will give you all that I can explain on paper of what I saw, and nothing more than I can help of what I thought.

Niagara!—the great, the glorious, the everlasting!—(that is, of things terrestrial, or rather *wat*errestrial), is situated just forty miles from Hamilton; and one fine day having nothing to do, it suddenly struck me that we hadn't been *there.*

Verily, how little we care to see what can be seen without trouble, however well worth seeing it be. A shopkeeper told me that he had been four years in Hamilton, and *thought* of going to Niagara, but had not been yet." However, we went ; and this is how we did it.

Started by train at six in the evening, and reached the " British," a small inn on the Canadian side of the Niagara Suspension Bridge, about eight. Oddly enough we found that one of the three landlords (brothers) had come out in the " Niagara" with us. Renewing a Niagara acquaintance at Niagara, eh ?—of course, he and they made us very comfortable. The large hotels were closed, as the summer company had dispersed to winter quarters some weeks since, so I cannot speak to their capabilities ; but can recommend the " British" to all small parties seeking shelter and civility, situated within four miles of the Falls, and commanding a fine view of the most beautiful suspension bridge in the world.

My never-satisfied reader will now be anticipating a graphic recital of how through the night I tossed, and could not sleep—my close proximity to the watery giant rendering me feverish and fanciful. Not a bit of it ! My last glass of whisky toddy was sufficiently potent to dispel the jumps, and though once in the night I *did* cock my ears, and ask myself whether Niagara was on the sea coast, I don't remember any other illusion or inconvenience, further than that of being awoke in the morning, some three hours earlier than had of late been my wont.

CHAPTER X,

NIAGARA.

IT was essentially a damp morning, but on being assured by the united voices of the landlords, backed by a very old inhabitant, that it was going to be a very fine day for the Falls, for the time of year, I awoke Lucille by playfully throwing a handful of pebbles against her window (the consequence of which cost me half a dollar); and in due time we found ourselves in high spirits and a seedy sort of char-a-banc, enjoying a drive on the Canadian side of the great —now rough, then smooth, and always soupy-looking river. Our driver, of course an Irishman, pointed out all the remarkable points. The only one which, however, I thought much of, and closely scrutinised, was where Blondin performed his tight-rope trip, backwards and forwards, and the more I looked at it the more I marvelled. My ejaculation of " Wonderful feat !" having been taken up by Paddy with, " Yes, an' the divil a shoe on them ayther, but baskets, the haythen !" summarily wound up my ocular and verbal remarks; and in a few moments, " Now, yer honner can see the smoke."

" The what ?"

" The smoke—the stame !"

" Ay, ay, I understand ; the steam of the boiling water, eh ?"

" *Bilin!* Divil a—— Ah ! yer honner's joking. Ha ! ha ! ha !"— and Paddy, as in duty bound, having slapped his thigh, and apparently nearly choked himself with his appreciation of my wit, proceeded to inform us that this " stame" was so thick sometimes, that ladies and gentlemen were wet through before they got within a mile of the " Shoe," which I didn't believe, and suggested the assistance of a shower of rain, which Paddy said was also " Plenty in them parts, by raison of the whirrlpull, bekase as how it drawd all the wather downnards !" With such like *discourse*, we soon found ourselves opposite the American

Falls, which, viewed from our side, looked insignificant to the eye that had in imagination pictured *what couldn't be.*

A few hundred yards further, and we pulled up opposite a tall white house, with an observatory on the top of it, and the Great Horse Shoe Fall, rumbling and tumbling within twenty feet of the door.

I never could describe anything—even things easy of description—so those of my readers who have been driving with me to Niagara, and want to know all about it, won't. Don't throw things about. Pick up the book again, and we'll see what we can do for you. Impatience.

You want to know about Niagara. Well, send to all the circulating libraries in your ken, and get all the works that treat upon the subject, read them all at the same time, occasionally varying the monotony of the employment by placing a few of them upside down, or crosswise, and commence the last page first, and you will know as much of Niagara when you have gone mad or asleep over the occupation, as you did before you began it, and as much as you are likely to know unless—you *see* it. There—it is the greatest jumble in creation. It took me but a few hours to get to it, and I havn't got back yet. I am at Niagara still! Don't tell me I can't hear the roaring, and the rumpus, and the riot. I tell you I *can*. Can't I see the glorious spray-bows! Can't I see the mad-cap waters—away—far off—miles!—coming on, laughing in the sunlight—laughing, dancing, shouting, jumping! Nearer, nearer—roaring—bounding! I had almost said *swearing*. Whirr-r-r —over she goes!—down—down! Oh, no, I can't see it—of course not. Hark back!

We hadn't been long at the " Shoe," and I hadn't had time to spend more than seventy dols. upon Indian fans, furs, bird-skins, beads, and such like useful and ornamental articles, when we were joined by Mr. *Eves*, a gentleman whose pleasant acquaintance we had cultivated at Hamilton, and who, taking compassion on our green and unprotected state, had followed to see us safely through the sights. I say *us*, though *I* did not benefit much by his kind attention—that commodity being exclusively lavished on Lucille, who, encouraged and supported by his experienced tongue, and stalwart arm, actually approached an inch and a half nearer to the edges of the various abysses than she otherwise

would. Well, we have seen the Horse Shoe Fall from the top — *I'm* off
to investigate the bottom ; and tearing myself away from my party,
with many expressed wishes from Lucille that I wouldn't, and uuex-
pressed ones from our Cicerone that I *would,* I descended to the foot of
the watery Pandemomium, and arraying myself in a suit of waterproof,
I proceeded with a guide to go underneath the fall.

Now, look here, reader ; I am not a man given to pulling up when
I have once started, nor do I *think* I lack my proper share of pluck ;
but, upon my honour, when I found myself crawling along a slimy ledge,
with nothing to hold on by but my eyelids, within a few feet of a Mammoth cauldron of mad, ginger-beer-like, unmanufactured-meerschaum-
looking liquid, and a solid green wall of ten thousand tons of glancing,
sparkling, dazzling water, falling within a few inches of my nose, my
own absurd smallness became momentarily so uncomfortably apparent,
that I thereupon set such an inconceivable amount of value on what
there was of me, my whole, sole, and only thought was, " If ever I get
safely out of this, you'll never catch me in it again !" And having
penetrated as far as the guide, in dumb show, informed me, anybody
goes, I slipped, sidled, and finally sloped back to my party ; and after
partaking of as stiff a jorum of—well, they called it *brandy* and water—
as ever was concocted, I declared myself ready to lead on or follow
wherever our friend suggested, *this* time determining he should be *my*
companion in all future explorings. What did I want him for ? Never
you mind. I had my reasons.

We drove back to our hotel, stopping by the way at Booth's Museum,
where, if any of my readers ever go, they will spend a very pleasant
hour or so, and a very great number of dollars if they are curiosity
hunting. Mr. Booth is a curiosity in himself—i.e., he is moderate in
his charges, and genuine in his articles, withal civil and obliging to
purchasers, and those who only come to " pull his things about."

I increased my expenditure considerably here, of course ; Booth's
Museum is about half way on the right hand side between Niagara
Bridge and the Falls.

When we returned to the " British" we had a big lunch, and I never
drank so much intoxicating liquid in my life in so short a sitting,

Lucille said I should be muzzy ; but did you ever, my dear sir, feel in that semi-excited, semi-sleepy, wholly don't-carish condition, a buoyancy in the heart and elasticity in the head, as if the two but required any amount of liquor to make them *hooroosh* together, and go in at anything—getting drunk was an improbability, if you *have*, you know, my sensation, after returning from the *watery landscape* I have just attempted in my own way to describe. After lunch we started over the suspension bridge for the American side of the river.

The suspension bridge; I should like to stop in the middle of it, and ask a question or two. Reader, did you ever see a bridge anywhere in your travels that you could sit down midway on it, or at both ends— I mean one after the other, and then go down underneath it, and then wish for a balloon to go up *over* it, and forget all about breakfast and dinner, and supper, and politics, and not care for anything but the bridge, for——well, ever so long, and get up early the next morning, after a hard day's work, to go and have a quiet look at a bridge—any bridge you have ever seen. If you *have* done this much, you needn't come to Niagara, because it would be tedious to have to do it all over again.

Can't I draw ? Of course I can draw ; but I cannot draw either Niagara Falls, or Niagara Suspension Bridge. No more could you, or anyone else that ever *drawd*, and do them justice.

The American side is, in my opinion, far the prettiest drive, and the view of the Falls from Goat Island, the finest. I did enjoy myself. *Eves*, who had seen everything a hundred times, and lost his eye for the magnificent, contented himself with feasting the same upon what he considered better worth looking at, and *he* enjoyed *him*self. Lucille was frightened to death every five minutes, lest the earth should give way under her, or that I should tumble into the water, and enjoyed *her*self. We meditated a further outlay at a curiosity shop kept by a turnpike man, on the bridge over the Rapids, but this individual's exceeding amount of Yankee impudence tied up our purse-strings, and we went home, suffering much from high spirits and bodily fatigue. By-the-bye, Grantley Berkeley was " doing the Falls" on the same day as ourselves, and I wrote my name in the Visitors' Book on Goat Island, immediately underneath his. There s a chance for autograph collectors !

One day at Niagara is the same as another, weather permitting, unless you tumble in, or something of the kind happens to damp your ardour —so, having given you a sample, I will not stop at Niagara any longer, but, hurry back to Hamilton, pay my bill, have a final chaff with the doctor, and off we go, our destination being Ottowa, the chosen site of the New House of Parliament. I forgot to say that while at Hamilton we journeyed to a place called St. Catherine's, a cold-water-cure spa, about twenty miles off, and there gave an entertainment to the most queer of all queer audiences. The proprietor, a Mr. (or, as they called him, *Colonel*) Stevenson, gave us the use of the room (his dining-room) *gratis*, and our stage consisted of all the dining tables put together at the end of the room, with a perilous centre entrance from the *"washing up"* regions *beyant*, by means of two ice-pails and a knife-board. We dressed in our private rooms for the commencement of the piece, and being ready in good time, I betook myself downstairs to see that all was right for Lucille's and my own quick changes ; while so occupied, Stocks came to me, and with a preliminary and unusual grin, said—

" You'll have to be very funny to-night, sir ; I never see such a rum set. They all got one foot in the grave, and the other in bandages ! There's an old gout has got three blackies to carry him down, and he's got a thing like a brass blunderbuss put to his ear, and they'll have to tell him what you say ; and there's a lady all rolled up in a blanket, and she's a going to sit close alongside of the stage to be out of the draught, and—" here I was obliged to cut his catalogue of eccentricities, in order to prepare Lucille for the sight, knowing the abilities of her risible muscles, when anything ridiculous in the audience catches her eye while acting. We had a very full room, nearly all ladies, always (I hope to be forgiven) a most unpleasant audience, especially if the actress be pretty, and the actor so intent upon himself and *his* business, to care about them on theirs.

After the performance was over, and the debtor and creditor account " totled" up, I found that *Colonel* Stevenson though charging nothing for *the* room, made up for his munificence by piling up his bill, and sticking me in *five dollars* for gas · the very outside extra cost. must have been inside *fifty cents*.

I was so disgusted with this imposition, that though I had pro-grammes out for a second night, and people had taken their tickets, and it would have paid us to have played, I packed up; and when I should have been making my bow to the Stevenson House audience, we were quietly enjoying our dinners in Hamilton.

From Hamilton we went to London; but both Lucille and myself having colds, and not liking the aspect of "things in general," we dropped the professional for awhile, and dined at seven o'clock, and ate cheese and vegetables, and walked about without being stared at, the same as other people.

We stayed one night at Port Hope on our way to Ottowa, and, much to my displeasure, I found that my original quarters were the only ones that I could put up at, the opposition house being closed for repairs. I have heard since, that this place and its proprietor have "shut up," which I sincerely trust may be the fate of a few others, my limits prevent me from noticing which, both house and landlord, instead of being a blessing to the weary and confiding traveller, are gross impositions, a "delusion and a snare." We arrived at the Pres-cott Junction, where the line branches off for Ottowa, at an early hour on a bitterly cold morning. We were tired, and preferred chancing a part night's rest to an entire night's railway shaking, and suffered by our preference. Don't ye, Oh my followers, do likewise!

Unpromising as the "house of call" was externally, its interior arrangements were even more unprepossessing still. Beds there were, and a roof, and beer, and——well, there, I don't *know* what Heenan's eyes were like, when he left off with Sayers, but he couldn't have been more blind than was I when I essayed to look at my watch, after having suffered excruciating torture for some five hours, and thought it "time to get up." However, "it is an ill wind," &c., &c.—as was shown as follows. Having contrived to prop one eyelid open, and thereby managed to manœuvre myself into my clothes, I went down in no very agreeable state of mind and body, you may be sure, and on presenting myself before the landlord of the so-called hotel (an enormous Irishman), ere I could give vent to my feelings, as I intended, I was greeted with

" By the powers !—but they've bin and sarved you shameful ! Come here, man !"   And before I knew what he was up to, I found my head grasped in one hand, while with the other, he knocked out the ashes of his pipe upon the table, and in an inconceivable short time manufactured a sort of mercurial-looking ointment, by means of ——you may guess what; and, in spite of my struggles, plentifully applied, and rubbed in, the pleasant compound into my eyebrows, cheeks, and forehead, then releasing me with a jerk, and surveying his manipulation with a grin of satisfaction, he said, " There let it bide, if ye plaze, and ye'll be sound as an apple in five minutes."   This prophecy proved correct, and I thereby profited in the possession of a valuable recipe, which since (self-mixed, and self-applied), I have never known in similar, or cases of mosquito, gnat, or nettle sting, to fail.

One other, and pleasanter little circumstance connected with Prescott, I deem worth mentioning—viz., that just previously to leaving, I purchased in the smallest tobacconist's shop I ever saw, some of the finest tobacco I ever smoked.   It bore the funny name of " *Billy Bowlegs.*"   I have never been able to get the identical stuff since, and herein make honourable mention of it, and weep its absence.

We reached Ottowa about four o'clock in the afternoon, and, for the first time in Canada, travelled in a coach without wheels ; the ground was covered with snow, and every conveyance was converted into a sleigh.   Lucille's only expressed remark on the subject was, that it " bumped awfully."   We arrived, without adventure or mishap, at " The George" (I think), a very old-fashioned English-looking inn (as " Georges" mostly are everywhere), where we were met by one Jos. Lee, a friend of our friend, Captain B., of quondam mention—an Englishman, something in the Customs, a *soi-disant* actor, and present proprietor of the theatre, which was just built and not yet opened, a particularly gentlemanly "jolly" fellow.   I had written to him to do the necessary for me, in the billing and posting, &c., and he had spared no pains to make the thing public.   He had rented a sort of chapel for us—that is, it had been a chapel, and was now a Sunday-school and *concert-room*, and a very uncomfortable-looking concern.   However, it was " Hobson's choice—that or none"—therefore we played therein, and and when, from the dens where we dressed (I thought at one time that Lncille was practising the cachuca, her chattering teeth doing the castanets, and her feet beating time), I heard the clatter of *hoofs* and a hum of voices, I vowed I would not again believe in appearances. The hall was quite full, and with an audience determined to be pleased. The second night it was crowded, and I was savage that I had taken the advice of (of course) good authority to " only play two nights, as the people were very slow there, and wouldn't stand more."

I verily believe we might have done *good business* for a fortnight, as I had not been idle with my pen, and we now boasted three distinct entertainments. However, we had made engagements to appear at Montreal and Quebec, and could not stay.

We devoted our last unoccupied day to a drive to the Falls, and other sights round and about the city. The Falls (as we saw them) are in many respects much more beautiful and interesting than Niagara.

The day was intensely cold, but bright and sunny. There were rocks and cones of solid ice of most fantastic shapes, and a myriad of Koh-i-noors could not have equalled the beauty of the prismatic colouring. The height of the Falls is, of course, nothing equal to Niagara, nor the volume of the water nearly so great ; but I felt more excitement, inasmuch that while the latter occasions a solemn wonder at its falling masses, which look as if they would continue to fall in the same direction, with the same regularity and the same sound, until Doomsday, the Ottawas are perpetually startling you with the idea that in their uproarious wildness, they'll make a rush at you, or turn round, and run sowewhere else, or do something that water never did before ; and, as you may have remarked, while listening to some swollen mountain torrent in the still night, the roar and rush *rise* and *fall* upon the ear—now loud, now dying away, and at irregular intervals ; so do the Falls of Ottowa—only, of course, magnified many thousand degrees. But then, as I said before, I cannot do the descriptive ; so, if my readers know no more of the Ottowa Falls than they did before, I can't help it,

A tremandous snow-storm came on about four in the afternoon, and effectually stopped our wanderings, but not before we had visited the site of the new Parliament Buildings : and I had time to decide that a lovelier spot was not to be found in all Canada ; and if *neutral* ground is an object with the powers that be, they have dropped upon it, and no mistake, for it would take a clever geographer to say whether the same stands in Upper or Lower Canada. Had I time, I here feel inclined to go in at a little bit of politics, but possibly I might put my foot in it, so I will content myself with saying that the present feelings of the *two* Canadas towards each other must not, and *cannot, continue.* There will be a row, and North America loveth us not. Unity is strength, &c., &c. Do you know what I would do if I were——somebody ? I would do away with the present tin-pot show of Government, and make a *Regency* of Canada. Why not ? Take the vote of every *landowner* and *house-holder* of all grades in Upper and Lower Canada, and know then the opinion of those whose opinion is only worth knowing. There is a growing Republicanism, and a bastard *Americanism,* in our English Canada, that may " put us up a tree" if left to fatten on its own *free* filth and come to maturity, while we thought it yet in its cradle. Hoop-de-dooden-doo ! There's a bit of politics, in spite of myself.

CHAPTER XI.

ONCE more in Montreal, and once more before an admiring audience; this time with proper preliminary notice and previous fame. Again, we were indebted to Mr. Nordheimer's kind consideration, to the leniency of the press, and the appreciation of the public. St. Andrew's Festival was celebrated here during our stay, and, in compliance to the wishes expressed to us by a deputation of the St. Andrew's committee, we postponed our last performance to give our services *for a song* (literally and figuratively) at the City Hall, an enormous edifice, on this occasion crowded to suffocation with the aristocracy and tag-rag and bob-tail of Canadian canny Scotland. Lucille sang "Annie Laurie," for the Scotchmen, and " Robert toi qui j'aime," for the Frenchmen (in which, as I said before, Montreal abounds); and I sang " The Maple Leaf," a Canadian national song, to the twain. We gained many laurels and a few dollars by the transaction, and shortly bade farewell, a long farewell, to tin-topped Montreal. I did not leave our friend, M., and Mr. Nordheimer, and the St. Lawrence Hall, without regret. We did return for a few hours, *en route* for New York, but few knew it, and I scarcely had time to say again, good-bye, though I shall have, in its proper place, to recount the only really perilous adventure we underwent in the course of our journey, as occurring on our final departure from Montreal.

Our second sojourn at Quebec, though it extended over five weeks, was unmarked by much incident; the snow now covered the ground with a solid cake of purest whiteness, to the depth of some six or seven feet. Oh, you don't believe it ! Well, ask anyone who has been in Canada, how long it takes to do *that*, with a continuous fall and a steady north-east wind, with the thermometer ten below Zero, and he or they will answer, " About five days," or I am no true historian. Blocks of ice, of acres in size, and four, five, and six feet in thickness, rammed, jammed, and dam—(I am not swearing), *dammed* up the great rapid river. Sleighing and tobogging, form the only amusement at this season ; the latter-named, being one of the oddest pastimes for adults I know of.   It consists in a lady or gentleman dragging a plank of wood, turned up like a skate at one end, to the top of a steep snowy incline— then, seating themselves thereon, the lady in front (coudled between the gentleman's legs), and sliding down to the bottom, at which happy termination, in nine cases out of ten, the concern capsizes, and the lady and gentleman, after an exciting struggle in the soft snow (the lady has generally three or four pairs of trousers on, so it don't matter), get up convulsed with laughter, and—do it all over again.

We gave two farewell performances at Quebec, and, this time, had my own money-taker, much to the evident chagrin of the lessee of the Hall, who officiated as such on the former occasion.   But Stocks had now, by experience, " got up" in the business, and having been done, in one or two instances, by unscrupulous *bogus** money passers, was now as 'cute as the 'cutest.   Mr. W., having no longer any, or at all events, as much, *interest*, in the affair as formerly, I regret to say behaved somewhat shabbily, and threw many impediments in our way ; and I unhesitatingly warn my followers, should they use this Hall, to be cautious in the framing of their agreement.

The entertainments were well attended, and from hence I transmitted my final balance-sheet to England, showing a clear *gain* of £500, achieved in little over six months, and almost solely by the representation of the productions of works of my own pen ; by sale of songs of my own composition, and books of entertainment of my own writing. Here, also, I showed the manuscript of a portion of this little narrative, and received a tempting offer from a speculative publisher for the copyright of the same, in Canada, which doubtless I might, had I needed it, have included in my honest gains, by my " *talent, as actor, singer, author, and composer.*"   However, as there were one or two "items in my account" that I thought might be objected to, I determined not to slacken in my labours, and after a somewhat wearisome stay at the " Clarendon" (which made a hole in a full purse—Go not *there !*) in Quebec, we bade adieu to the scene of the immortal Woolfe's victory and death, and turned our faces southward to New York, *viâ* Montreal.

---

* A Yankee term for " sham."

We had an exciting passage across the river to Point Levi ; but thanks to the kind assistance of a gentleman (who, I suppose, will forgive me for here giviug his name to the world—ahem ! though I did not ask his permission, as one of the select few of jolly good fellows mentioned in this highly-meritorious work) we surmounted all difficulties without further inconvenience than was consequent upon the uproarious laughter in which we were compelled to indulge. We crossed in a large flat-bottomed canoe, steered by our friend *Charlton*, and propelled by eight stalwart Canadian boatmen, sometimes high and dry on a huge block of ice, when the crew were out in an instant, and swimming, wading, or struggling in all shapes and ways, they pulled and pushed the canoe as if it were a sleigh until it went plump into the water again. Then, such duckings and splashings to regain their seats—then, out oars, and away we would go some hundred yards, and shoot into a little creek just wide enough for one boat's width, when we did a little bit of punting with long iron-spiked poles—Charlton watching every inlet and outlet, as only one who had crossed in a similar fashion hundreds of times *could* do, and steering with consummate nicety. The ice on either side towered some five or six feet, so that occasionally he would jump out, much to Lucille's horror, as he said, '' to take the bearings," and in again like a cat, with a " shove her along !—now she goes !—now she don't !—out again, boys !—Lord, there's the water got into my boots ! Miss Lucille, what are you laughing at ?" It took us three quarters of-an-hour to do this *amphibious* (I know the term is wrong, but never mind) journey, but with worse luck and less experienced men, passengers are sometimes four or five hours out; indeed, Stocks with the luggage, though he started an hour before, arrived, with his ears frost-bitten, half-an-hour after us.

We had to stay the night at a sort of *shebeen shop,* apology for a public house, and here a slight adventure must be chronicled, as it tended to the enlargement of our little party. Lucille *would* have with her, as her constant companion, a hermetically-sealed-to-all-but-herself, bag—*what was* in it *I* never to this day, knew. This bag was my positive plague ; in railway carriages, boats, and bed-rooms, it was

always "*left behind again !*"—and, of course, poor Pill Garlick had to
send, go, or in some way retrieve said bag, often to the losing of a
train or boat, and always to the ditto of my otherwise excellent
temper.   On the present occasion when we had, as I thought, shaken
ourselves down for the night, and I was enjoying in anticipation the
demolition of a beef-steak—the perfume of the *trimmings* of which
already pervaded our apartment—I was horror-stricken on hearing a
familiar voice, exclaim, in semi-angry accents, " Now, *ma*, you have
never *gone and done* it again ?"

I knew, instanter, what that meant. That blessed bag was left at the
railway station, or *depôt*, and, of course, (Stocks being out on some
business or other), off I started (distance, little short of a mile) be-
moaning the certain ruin of the steak, and mentally bestowing every
species of abuse upon the wretched bag. Arrived at the depôt, I discovered
in the doubtful light the " left luggage" room ; I "pulled the bobbin,
and up went the latch"—an oil lamp, nearly out, was on a table in the
centre of the barn-like apartment, and all round and about was strewed
and stored an indescribable confusion of " left" and right luggage.

"Anyone here?"

Echo answered "nobody," which I thought irregular to say the
least of it. I took a turn round, and, " the saints be praised!
here's the —— bag !" I delightedly and audibly exclaimed, clutching
the article and turning to depart rejoicing. A deep growl—deep,
determined, and distractingly close to my dexter calf—made me drop
the article like a hot potato, and I immediately became aware of the
presence of a pair of " glowing orbs," which experience warned me were
the property of a large animal of the canine species, lying crouched
beneath the afore-mentioned table. I thought I would put the door
between me and possible danger, and with that praiseworthy and
prudent intent, I *backed* towards the door, when, to my horror, that
wretched contrivance, seized by a wicked whim, or a gust of wind,
suddenly slammed to—the *beast* sprang from underneath the table,
capsizing the same and extinguishing the light, and in less than *no
time* I felt a sharp cut on my face, a pair of heavy paws upon my
shoulders, and over we went, hitting my head a nasty knock in my

descent against a particular sharp corner of something or other. I was uppermost, *that* was something—I held on like grim Death to what seemed to me an animated door-mat; and didn't I " holloa ?"—Rather !

" Now then, what's up ?—jist hold on, young 'un, till I come ! Darn it, whar's the glim ?"

" Hang the glim !" I said, blowing like a grampus, and not a little frightened, too, " call your confounded dog away !—or I'll throttle him, by G—d !"

" No fear of that, lad !" was the new comer's pleasant reply ; " look out for thee own wizen, thee's cotched a Tartar this journey !—that's fact !"

" Don't be a fool !" I exclaimed, feeling that my fingers had not the slightest effect upon the brute's throat, and *feeling* also that I was bleeding. " I am no thief, but a traveller ; and if you don't come here instantly, I'll *shoot* the dog, and you, too !"

This bloodthirsty threat had its effect ; he spoke to the dog, and snapped a match on the wall. The dog left me with a low growl of disappointed defiance, and his owner examined me, holding the light above his head.

" Confound you, for a stupid ass !" I savagely exclaimed, " can't you see that beast has bitten me ?"

"An' sarve you right ! What wur you doing in this—— ?"

I rapidly explained the circumstance, and the custodian of stray carpet bags forthwith altered his tone—" The dog was raised on the premises, and know'd as well as a Christian everybody that com'd near the place, and hop'd I wasn't hurt," which I was, for the animal's tooth or teeth had just caught the bridge of my nose and my cheek-bone, almost laying bare the latter. Some cold water and sticking plaister soon allayed and patched up the wounds, and then I spoke, " I must have that dog !"

" Well, I guess, you oughter had enough of him !"

" Will you sell him ?"

" No."

" Then I shall kill him !"

" Will ye ?"

My answer was the sudden production of a small revolver, *unloaded.*

" Hut, tut—hold on ! Ye want to buy, 'cause the beast's a bitten ye ?"

" Yes."

" What'll ye give ?"

" What do you ask ?"

" Say, twenty dollars."

" There's the money."

" Well, now, the missus 'll be precious savage—but twenty dollars, twenty dollars !—that's fact !   Whar do ye live ?"

" Come along, and I'll show you."

A glass of whisky to the master, and a plate of meat to the animal half-an-hour after, made all friendlily disposed to each other, and from then I became owner of the splendid animal that has since been my constant companion, Lucille's *great* pet, and the original of the accompanying sketch.

It may, perhaps, not be out of order at this portion of my little history, to devote a page (contrary to my intentions at starting on my literary effort) to a table of distances and first and second-class fares from Quebec, to such towns as I consider, from experience and hearsay, eligible for Entertainment purposes. In most of them I have been myself, but owing to no agent in advance, I was obliged to pass through, and thereby lost many opportunities.

"NOW THEN, WHAT DO YOU WANT?"

ROUTES, DISTANCES, AND FARES BY RAILWAY AND STEAMER FROM QUEBEC:—

TOWNS.	MILES.	FARES BY RAIL OR STEAMER.		ROUTE.
		DOLS. CENTS.	DOLS. CENTS.	
Belleville	388	10 35	3 50	Grand Trunk Railway or Steamer.
Brockville	293	7 00	3 00	Grand Trunk Railway or Steamer.
Cobourg	431	11 75	4 50	Grand Trunk Railway or Steamer.
Guelph	550	14 50	6 00	Grand Trunk Railway.
Hamilton	539	11 00	5 00	Grand Trunk Railway or Steamer.
Kingston	340	7 75	3 75	Grand Trunk Railway or Steamer.
*London	615	16 35	6 75	Grand Trunk Railway.
Montreal	168	3 00	1 00	Grand Trunk Railway or Steamer.
Niagara	537	12 00	5 50	Great Western Railway or Steamer, viá Toronto.
Ottawa	335	7 00	3 50	Viá Prescott.
Peterborough	459	10 75	5 50	Viá Port Hope.
Port Hope	437	12 00	4 50	Grand Trunk Railway or Steamer.
St. Catharines	560	12 00	5 50	Great Western Railway from Hamilton.
Toronto	500	11 00	5 00	Grand Trunk Railway or Steamer.
Williamsburg	260	6 00	2 75	Grand Trunk Railway or Steamer.

Value of English Money throughout Canada.

							DOLS. CENTS.
One Sovereign	...	...	...	£1 4 0 currency, or			4 85
One Crown	...	...	...	0 6 1	„	1	20
One Shilling	...	...	...	0 1 3	„	1	20

I also here am tempted to append a route for a yachting tour, originally compiled for my own private and especial usage and benefit, but now, upon "second thoughts," unselfishly given to all whom it may concern, with a thorough conviction that should any enterprising Yachtsman take the trip, he will return much gratified with the same, and grateful to me.

QUEBEC TO MONTREAL.	By the River St. Lawrence, distance 189 miles; good navigation for vessels drawing 20 feet of water.
MONTREAL TO KINGSTON.	By the River St. Lawrence, distance 200 miles. Passing round the rapids by Canals, four in number, the whole looks about 35 miles, and navigable for vessels drawing 8 feet, the locks being 210 feet long, and 50 ft. wide. Sixty miles below Kingston commences the Lake of the Thousand Islands, where good fishing will be found.
KINGSTON TO PORT DALHOUSIE.	By Lake Ontario, distance 225 miles.
PORT DALHOUSIE TO PORT COLBORNE.	By the Willand Canal, distance 28 miles, navigable for vessels drawing 9 feet water, the locks being 150 long and 26 feet wide. Niagara Falls 12 miles distant from Port Dalhousie.

PORT COLBORNE TO DETROIT	By Lake Eni, distance 300 miles thence, or by Detroit River, distance 25 miles.
DETROIT TO PORT SARNIA.	By Lake St. Clair, distance 20 miles, and River St. Clair, distance 40 miles.
PORT SARNIA TO SAULT ST. MARIE.	By Lake Stawn, crossed by Georgian Bay a distance of 500 miles. Georgian Bay abounds in fish, and is of the same character of scenery as the Lake of the Thousand Islands, but much greater in extent—about 150 miles long and 100 miles wide—containing upwards of 20,000 Islands and Inlets.
SAULT ST. MAIN TO FORT WILLIAM AND SUPERIOR CITY.	By the north shore of Lake Superior, where will be found the best fishing in America. Distance to Fort William 250 miles; thence to Superior City, 150 miles.

Tug Steamers will be found at all places when the wind may render it desirable to employ them, in Canals, Rivers, &c.

Bayfield's Charts (which are remarkably correct) of the whole of the foregoing route, excepting the Canals, may be had at Potter's, in the Poultry, London.

The St. Lawrence, between Longueil and Montreal, had been frozen over many weeks, and there had been symptoms for some days past of the ice breaking up.   On the morning of our starting from Montreal, I was making a hurried breakfast, when Stocks (who, I had hoped, was midway across the river with the baggage) came to me, and said he "couldn't get no such thing as a sleigh to cross, 'cos it had been 'nounced dangerous." I asked him how the mails were going (as it was the mail-train we meant travelling by), and, he replied, *he* "didn't know, but sposed somehow." "Well," I answered, "*we* will go *somehow*, too !" And somehow we did.

I packed off Stocks, bag and baggage, in the mail omnibus, thinking he might feel himself glorified in perishing (if there *was* to be any perishing) with her Majesty's mail bags, and forthwith sought a conveyance for ourselves, which I had some difficulty in obtaining, they all refusing to cross the river, excepting some miles round by Point St. Charles. At last, I engaged a big-whiskered Scotchman and his "cuckoo," for the consideration of five dollars, to get us to Longueil, the best way he could, in time for the train.

After about ten minutes of the ordinary amount of bumping, an *extra*ordinary quantity of the same induced me to put my head out of the window, when I discovered that Scotchy, after all, was taking the short-cut across the river, and the unevenness of the ice corroborated what had been told me of the probability of a speedy "break up." I did not tell Lucille or her mother of this immediately, but the jumping and jolting became every moment so much greater, and our progress, in proportion, so much slower, that the fact was soon patent to all, and the alarm consequently unmistakeable. The track was marked by branches of trees, stuck up on either side at intervals of about one hundred yards, and the oozing of the water through the holes in which they were placed, was ominous. We were now about midway, and the fissures—yes, *fissures*, reader—becoming wider and more frequent, I began to think I ought to comply with Lucille's terrified entreaty to "turn back," and communicated our desire to Scotchy. What was our surprise on hearing him reply, "Na, ye canna turn back—we maun mak' the beest of a bad beesness; hauld oop !" This last to the horse, who at the moment dropped his hind legs into a crack, and didn't seem able to get them out again.

To add to our miseries and difficulties, a blinding storm of sleet now came on, and the *bellying* and cracking of the ice under us was really alarming. Keeping our seats was impossible. Had the sleigh been an open one, I would not have so much cared, as in the event of its *going through*, the danger of which was now imminent, I might have thrown the *feminines* out on the broken ice, and held them safe until help arrived. As it was, we should have gone down like squirrels in a cage.

Of course, everybody knows we were *not* drowned, so I will make my story short by saying that we eventually got on to sound ice in shallow water, and thence on shore to receive quite an ovation from a large crowd who had assembled and watched our dangerous voyage, almost from its commencement. We were the last that crossed, and in an hour the *mail road* was a confused mass of rough waves and rugged blocks of floating ice. "All's well that ends well," and so ends this Chapter.

CHAPTER XII.

FROM Montreal to New York was the most interesting road we had yet travelled. Lovely country, fine rivers, large towns, and wonderful bridges. We stayed a night at the *Troy House*, in Troy, a very clean and handsome-looking town. I made all necessary inquiries with regard to giving our Entertainment there in the course of a few weeks, and found the *newspapers* well inclined to help me. To one gentleman connected with the press of Troy, I candidly communicated my doubts of success, after the way in which the New York papers had treated me. His answer was, " New York is not America ; and it has of late usurped such self-supremacy, that in four cases out of five what they write up, the press of other cities write down, out of sheer opposition." And he gave me several instances of tremendous hits in New York, failing to make any impression in Boston, Philadelphia, and other places.

I was much struck by the superiority of the " turn-outs" in this town to those I had yet seen anywhere else. Of course, all the carriages were sleighs, as even here the snow was several inches thick ; but the horses and harness were unexceptionable, and the fur robes and trimmings very handsome. We left Troy with the determination of returning at a future day.

Again in New York, after an absence of nearly seven months. Anything more disgusting than the state of the streets I never saw. London, after a week of November rain and fog, was never in such a pickle. The *brilliant* Broadway was (I do not exaggerate) knee-deep in mud and slush ; the omnibuses, in order to bring about this agreeable state of things, and to prevent the hack sleighs from taking from *them* any portion of their human traffic, carry with them bags of salt, which, as fast as snow falls, and shows a disposition of hardening, they literally shower over it—the effect of which, anybody chemically informed, will know ; and the uninformed, from the foregoing lines, will guess.

This time we put up at a house kept by an Englishman, in Princes-street, and were tolerably comfortable, having a private sitting-room, and our meals served therein, in proper English fashion. Considering my wager won, and myself as no longer under the ban of *incognito*, I now made a point of seeing and introducing myself to everybody who had shown the least disposition to befriend the " Amateur," and in a short time made arrangements with the proprietors of the Hope Chapel Hall, *on* Broadway, for a series of entertainments, and though my old enemies still showed their venom in " faint praise," I soon found that I could hold my own in New York, and the " Programme" (the American *Era*) thus spoke of us .—

" CAPTAIN MORTON PRICE AND MISS CATHARINE LUCETTE.—This gentleman, whose real name *is* Horton Rhys, and turns out to be really an Amateur, of which, on his former visit to New York, we reasonably had, and expressed, our doubts, has now located himself at the Hope Chapel Hall, and, with his fair and accomplished ally, is giving a series of the entertainments with which he seems to have made a most successful tour through the Canadas. We dropped in last evening, and found the room fully and fashionably attended, and, contrary to our intentions, we found attraction sufficient to detain us to the close of the performance, which in all respects, is worthy a visit from all who delight in good English music, and more than ordinary good acting."

This was a turn round, and no mistake. The other papers, with a few exceptions, followed suit ; and I would here tender my thanks to *Wilkes' Spirit of the Times* for the uniform kindness and support I received from that journal (the American *Bell's Life*). There *is* another sporting paper, 'yclept *The Clipper,* which, to the *Spirit,* is, as the *Telegraph* to the *Times,* and to whose uniform malignity, I shall ever " *owe one.*" About this time, the coming great fight for the champion-ship, between Heenan and Tom Sayers, engrossed the thoughts and conversation of all classes in New York, and I soon got into hot water by the *too* (for my own health) free expression of my opinions thereon, and other *international* matters.

The Americans were still smarting under the defeat inflicted on them by the English Cricketers, and seemed to look forward to this fight to

recover their lost laurels.   Every paper, however previously peaceable
in deportment, had now sporting correspondence and pugilistic para-
graphs, and considerably " riled" at the bounce and balderdash contained
therein, I forthwith rushed into print, and fierce were the onslaughts
made on my " opinions" by sundry fire-eating pen-wielders. I will give
you, dear reader, a specimen to prove to you that to the best of my
single-handed power, I " stuck up" for the honour of " the old country."

LETTER FROM CANADA UPON THE ENGLISH CRICKETERS.

Apology for Julius Cæsar.

" Montreal, Jan. 10.

" MY DEAR SIR,—I have this day read in your SPIRIT of last week an
account of the dinner given to the English Cricketers at a ' hostelrie,'
in that hot-bed of cricketers, the county of Surrey, England.   You
have thought fit to bestow a cut from your editorial lash upon Julius
Cæsar for thus speaking in the opening of his speech on that occasion :
' They (the cricketers) certainly were received in Canada in a very kind
and hospitable manner, indeed, but he (J. C.) could not possibly say so
much for the United States.'   Will you allow me, an Englishman, to
say, or rather write, a few words upon the quoted sentence ?   I will
preface them with my own opinion of the same.   *It was a thought-*
less and unjustifiable statement, and I will tell you why : Julius Cæsar in
thus giving his opinion to the cricketing world of England, meant to
say that which he didn't ; he meant to complain of certain pecuniary
arrangements by which the pecuniary benefit which would have accrued
to him and his *confrères,* on the occasion of the third day's play, became
seriously lessened.   This, however, was no fault on the American side ;
it lay rather on that of the English.

"The gentleman who had the whole and sole management of the money
matters connected with the Eleven, should have thoroughly explained to
them the terms on which they took their benefit, before the benefit took
place. All would then have been well. They might have accepted
or refused the said benefit. I am not prepared to say he did not do so.
If he did, there must have been a great mistake on his part, or on that of
the American agent in the matter. This, however, smacks of mis-
management, but cannot hint at ' unkindness' or lack of ' hospitality.'
Those who heard J. Cæsar's speech (saving the Eleven themselves)

would not take it in that light. They (the guests and entertainers) would think they were not received in New York, Philadelphia, and Rochester as men should meet men speaking the same language as themselves, as cricketers should meet cricketers, as Americans should meet Englishmen. Therefore, do I raise my voice, or rather pen, ' unaccustomed as I am,' &c., &c., to refute the construction that most likely will be put upon the sentence in question ; and how can I do it better than by giving *verbatim* the opinion of two of the Eleven (their names are at your service if you want them, one was present at the banquet, the other was not), as to their reception and treatment by the New Yorkers?

" No. 1.—' Upon my soul, sir, we thought they never would have let us come away. Morning, noon, and night it was ' Where is P., where is L., where is J. ?' We were quite bored with their hospitality.'

"No. 2.—' Stand treat ? I don't think any one of us ever paid a copper, out of our own hotel, for either a drink or a smoke.'

" I shall be in England, wind and waves permitting, next Spring, and believe me it will be no fault of mine if one erroneous idea remains in the heart of any Englishman with regard to the treatment and reception of the English Eleven in America.

" Yours, dear sir, &c., &c.,   M "

LETTER FROM " MORTON PRICE."

Reply to "Veritas"—Heenan and Sayers—Umpire and the Derby— Devoy and Mitchell—Phelan, Roberts, and Berger, in the International Matches.

" My DEAR SIR,—I fear that my reply to ' Veritas,' in your edition of the 11th inst., must have in some way ' riled' that gentleman, as I find him using my name entire and by *instalments*, in his various pen-and-ink skirmishes, to such an extent, that I may shortly be expected to be looked upon as a species of ' household word' by those who read your correspondence. I don't object, but must here say it is not graceful or courteous to *call names!* Since last writing to you I have re-perused ' Veritas'' rejoinder, and take so much umbrage at one

sentence therein that I must quote it. It occurs half-way down his
first column, and runs thus : ' In the first place, his remark' (meaning
mine) ' implied—he' (meaning me) ' wishes it now to imply something
else—that superiority in height was a positive disadvantage to a man,
be he a good sparrer or bad—*vide* his article.' ' Veritas' here unjustly
undertakes to show a shuffle on my part, without the ghost of a pretence
for doing so. And, secondly, asserts that I have given to your readers
an opinion that would at once ' stamp me Goose,' and unworthy of a
place among the correspondents of the SPIRIT. If ' Veritas' can by
any possibility establish, from my words, or the tenour of my argument,
that ' *be he a good sparrer or bad*" was by me implied, I knock under
and hide my ' diminished head' at once and for ever. I based my
opinion as to Heenan's height being a disadvantage to him upon what
has been given to me as fact, by an experienced eye-witness of the
contest between him and Morrissey—viz., that when Morrissey succeeded in breaking through Heenan's guard, and getting home a heavy
blow, although Heenan was quite fresh, he couldn't keep his hands
down, his arms flew round wildly, and he was licked in five minutes, by
as many of Morrissey's rib-benders. Those of your readers who saw
the fight well know how near this is to truth ; and thus for the present
I will dismiss ' Veritas'' misconception and consequent mis-statement.
I do like your correspondent ' America ;' he does speak as if he would
stick to ' the Boy' to his last farthing, and if ' the Boy' should chance
to be beaten, would stick to him still. That's the sort of backer I like.
First knock down, first fall, first blood, and fight, all to be won nobly,
and patriotically. Hurrah ! ' A second Waterloo, in which two of the
greatest generals in the world ever produced are to contend.' That
simile I do not like, for, if I can credit my eyes and ears, this will be a
case of General against *no* General—a great cáptain at the head of
a smaller force of bone and muscle, size, weight, and sinew, against a newly-
appointed and inexperienced commander of a vastly greater strength of
the same commodity. Waterloo truly resembled this in all, but that
the Generals were equally well experienced, and the superiority in
quantity on one side was negatived by the quality on the other. This

may be a second Waterloo yet. And though I do not wish to enter into the lists in any way with 'America' (I mean your correspondent), excepting that of good fellowship, I must say, I think if he threw a little less nationality into his opinions, and left Paul Jones and his victories in British waters out of the argument, his letters would be accepted by both your American and English readers with much more pleasure. I do not think it can be the wish of either to create feelings of animosity in the coming contest. I say, Studiously avoid that! Remember, Heenan is now in the land of strangers, one of whom he is going to fight—not because he is an Englishman, but because he is the champion boxer of the world. Tom will think no more of Heenan's being an American than if he were a Frenchman or a Nigger ; he knows he has to fight, and lick if he can, a man a good deal bigger than himself, and that's all. I don't think Tom's historical and geographical recollections extend to a knowledge of the *locale* of English and American successes and defeats, and if you mentioned Paul Jones, he would probably ask ' What was his weight ?' But there are others of more education than Tom, who will read with displeasure such novel training instruction as that proffered by 'America' to Heenan—viz., ' Let him (that's ' the Boy') on some clear morning, climb to the top of some chalk cliff, &c., and call to mind the achievements of Paul Jones, &c., &c., &c.' The climbing I don't object to, but I feel assured that Heenan will have other things to think of than ' Paul Jones' when the event comes off, and I hope that no national war-cries will be heard or needed, to stimulate either combatants to greater ' deeds of daring.' I am, in a small way, doing my very best to bring about some far more interesting matches (at least I consider them so) than this of Sayers and Heenan. ' Veritas' laughs at my calling the coming contest between these boxers a fight with fists, between a big man and a little one ; but he cannot alter the fact any more than he can, that a large proportion of, at all events English, admirers of manly sports won't care a button which gets the worst of the pummelling. Should Umpire win the Derby, Epsom Downs will witness such a scene of enthusiasm as it never yet has done. I'll take odds both the horse and the jockey are carried back to the weighing stand. There will be 'Stripes-and-Stars' neck-ties, 'Umpire' coats, and 'Ten Broeck' hats. Such a triumph would, indeed, be a national one. The acknowledged best-looking three-year-old colt ever produced in America, against the pick of all England, carrying fair and even weights, equally well ridden, and equally well trained. The fight will not stand comparison with such a struggle. Well, supposing the battle over, and the Derby won, as fortune chooseth to decide those events, turn we now to the chances of the champion, Chambers, coming over here to try the great gun, Ward, in his own waters. I hope Mr. Wilkes, during his stay in England, will see the great sculler, though that is improbable, as Newcastle is a long way from London, and Chambers is a stay-at-home. However, express trains in England travel fifty miles an hour, and I don't expect Mr. W. will confine his English experiences to London. If he does see and speak to him, I think there will be no doubt as to the match coming off. I have written to Mr. Mitchell, the Racket Champion, to make a point of seeing Mr. W., who, by-the-bye, may have a chance of witnessing the match between Erwood and him, and will be able thereby to draw a line between Mr. M. and Devoy. I fear Roberts will not be induced to come!—he is similarly circum-stanced to Mr. Phelan, and don't care to leave his business to be managed by others. I opine he would be licked if he did, at the big ball game. However, if Mons. Berger will quit his titled and aristo-cratic friends and admirers for a short time, and condescend to accept 5,000 or 10,000 dollars, when he wins them, from the plebeian patrons of Michael Phelan, Mr. Roberts won't be needed to afford a rich treat to the lovers of billiards in New York. And now I must really wind up, hoping I have not trespassed too much on your valuable space, and believe me, "Yours truly, MORTON PRICE."

THE INTERNATIONAL MATCHES.

"Nothing extenuate, nor aught set down in malice."

TO THE EDITOR OF WILKES' "SPIRIT OF THE TIMES."

"DEAR SIR,—If you go on admitting everybody's letters into your paper respecting the anticipated trial of strength, skill, and pluck, 'yclept the 'Fight for the Championship,' you'll shortly have to enlarge the said paper considerably, and by way of contributing my mite towards so desirable an object, I beg to have the pleasure of sending for your consideration (and that of your readers, should you insert the same) *my opinion of and concerning international matches likely and unlikely to 'come off.'* First (and viewed in a belligerent light) most important on the list stands the fight for the Championship, now finally arranged to be 'called on' on the 16th of April next. Lots of people imagine this will be a great fight. *I don't.* Lots of people are going 'across' to see John Heenan whip, or be whipped (*Anglicè*, 'lick or be licked') by Tom Sayers. *I can't.* Lots of people are going to lose or win their (or other people's) money on the result. *I shan't.* My reasons for so determining may not be uninteresting, as they are unprejudiced, based on experience, and published for the benefit of those seeking information, but ignorant where to apply. Presuming your correspondents, ' F. F.' and ' J. A. D.' to be Americans, I must forthwith attack them for frightening the English P.R. patrons in New York in a most unwarrantable manner in your last number of the SPIRIT. The first states, speaking of Nat Langham, ' he compares unfavourably with Heenan in strength, science, or skill as a boxer.' The second, 'he is far inferior to Heenan in science, and the latter could easily drive him out of a ten-acre lot; Price, Coeburn, and others, &c., &c., can out-spar him.' This of *the acknowledged best English boxer of the day!* Were this the fact it would be indeed all U P. with the *little* champion ; but I say emphatically to those who would lay out their money *on facts, not fancies,* Don't believe it ! This may seem a rudeness to your correspondents ; it is not meant as such, but I say (looking to the SPIRIT and the correspondence therein, as New Yorkers and Old Yorkers, and middle-aged Yorkers *do* for guidance and information in the matter) such assertions as those of ' F. F.' and ' J. A. D.' are calculated to mislead and bias, rather than direct and caution.

I have seen Heenan box on two occasions. I have seen Sayers fight all his battles but the last; I backed him for all of them, but that with Langham. The latter's science at that period was superior to Sayers' ; at that time he was not (as your correspondents correctly state he *now* is) of

' sickly constitution,' or ' spare.' Tom Sayers' only conqueror was as near as possible 100 lb. of bone and muscle, like steel and whip-cord. Yet every man who witnessed the fight, and knows a tittle about fighting, feels assured that had Master Tom been five or six pounds lighter than he was—i.e., in better condition—he would have won. Therefore, I say, Don't—because your correspondents say they have seen Nat Langham (they have *not* seen *him*, they have seen his shadow), and that he is slim, sickly, &c., &c.—think, therefore, that Heenan must whip Sayers.

How Heenan stood up to Grantley Berkeley, 1 know not; he might have disguised his real fighting attitude for the reason ' G. B.' has assumed, but I have seen him spar when he was not aware of an Eng-lishman being present, and I echo the *baronet's* opinion, that if that is his attitude and those his tactics, that he will be licked as sure as his name is Heenan.   " Yours truly,   Morton Price."

————

I must also give you a specimen of my most-difficult-to-be-worsted opponent's style, and I think you will admit we were well matched :

LETTER FROM " VERITAS"—REPLY TO " MORTON PRICE."

" No Man's Land, Feb. 22nd.

" If there's a hole in a' your coats,
      I rede ye tent it ;
    A chiel's amang you takin' notes,
        An' faith he'll prent it."

" Dear Spirit,—You may perhaps call to mind an interrogatory that appeared frequently at the head of articles in the daily papers, a few years since, when the Rev. Ebenezer Williams, of Indian Missionary memory, was ' Heir apparent to the throne of France'—viz., " Have we a Bourbon among us ?" If we may be allowed, for a moment, to believe in the transmigration of souls, we may safely congratulate our-selves in having at the present time in our midst one of the famous sporting calebrities of the olden times—perhaps the founder of the ' Olympic Games,' who, having shifted his ' mortal coil' from one tenement to the other, has come down through many generations, and after appearing for a time as ' Pierce Egan,' or ' Mr. Jackson,' *aut quicunque alius*—easy of translation—has now deigned to appear to us once more under the guise and cognomen of ' Morton Price.' But, sir, whoever or whatever he may be, it must be evident to all unprejudiced persons that he is a real phenomenon in athletic literature—a perfect mass of ' experience' in all sporting matters—a conglomeration, if one may thus express it, of all the Nos. of *Bell's Life,* from the moment of its inception down to the present time ; and in our ring matters a volume of a new style of tactics, bound in ' sheep,' to which a ' certain Price' is affixed, but which is nevertheless free—(*Igitur gaudeamus*)—to all those " seeking information, but in ignorance where to apply." (N. B.—For the above Latin phrase, please overhaul the Psalms of David, and when found turn down a leaf !)

" Why, sir, his name should be embalmed in all our memories and handed down from father and son, to future generations of disenthralled Yankees, as the self-abnegating philanthropist, the very personification of disinterested benevolence, who, ' in spite of wind and weather,' dared to cross the stormy waters of the Atlantic—who knows but in mid-winter, without mittens—for the noble purpose of dispensing his exhaustless stores of *Priceless* intelligence to the American people, ' based' on the solid foundation of a long-tried experience. (Hear !) And, moreover, the author and getter-up of a series of grand tournaments, on American ground and water, of all the sports congenial to the disposition of two great peoples !

" Magnificent *ideah* ! and well worthy of the genius of its overwhelmingly renowned progenitor ! who, *en passant,* may be induced to enter for a prize in one or other of these tournaments, and having himself ' trained for a few four-mile rowing matches,' he will have an excellent opportunity to show up his artistic skill with an oar, or a pair of sculls, as M. Berger with his cue to gaping crowds of awe-struck greenhorns (*Anglicè,* muffs) ; and we shall thus see at rowing—as from the other ' at billiards'—' what we never yet beheld !' And as he will then have (' or think he has') ' two to one the best of it,' with the good fortune which is invariably the follower of skill and pluck, while teaching his Transatlantic cousins to skilfully toss an oar, he can with equal grace bestow a goodly pile of almighty dollars within his capacious breeches pockets. For, dear sir, although such a series of tournaments would undoubtedly be a splendid school for us degenerate sons of Britain's Isle, in enabling us to perfect ourselves in all the manly sports under the immediate supervision of ' Morton Price'—yet alas ! we must rest satisfied for the present with the glory of having contended with, and been well beaten by, men who cannot possibly be excelled by anyone anywhere—' out of England'—in any of the aforesaid sports. *J'ai fini. Nix cum arous.*

" There, dear SPIRIT, if you and your readers are not now ' astonished at the power of my elbow,' I beg to assure you all that I myself am perfectly exhausted by the immense draft the above effusion has made at sight upon the previously diminished resources of my brain. (I shall have to take a sea voyage to recuperate.)

" It was managed, however, with strong coffee, and has the merit of being, with a few exceptions, quite original. But as I had somehow, very unfortunately, mislaid my ' French and Spanish made easy,' and ' Morton's last,' containing literally nothing worth stealing, I was obliged, from dire necessity, as from strong habit, to substitute a passage from Burns, and one line from an old song we used to sing at sea sometimes, in 'spite of wind and waves.'

" I luckily tumbled upon an antique copy of Burns, to my great joy, in the corner of the garret, while frantically endeavouring to repair my severe ' foreign loss' as above stated. One word for my Latin phrases, which I am happy to know this person has sufficient intelligence to understand. They were imported from Oxford direct, *per mea propria, persona,* expressly for WILKES' SPIRIT OF THE TIMES, and were intended to be so simple and easy of translation, that ' he who runs'—or rows —' might read,' ' and the wayfaring man, though a fool (I should judge he was a sensible person) might not err therein.'

" The only excuse I can offer for appropriating more than half a column of the SPIRIT (one and a quarter columns appears to be his particular aversion), is the rush of ideas, over which the hand has no control. And that reminds me that to obviate so terrible an evil this time, I must 'fetch up all standing,' 'take a severe turn,' 'clap on stoppers,' 'nipper well,' and 'hold on hard.' I will only say that I am rejoiced that this person finds my 'counters' 'harmless,' which is entirely owing to my being a trifle over six feet (and I will add, perhaps, to my future benefit, well proportioned), and that I have not as yet learned to 'hit low.' But as he considers height a 'positive disadvantage,' he of course has no cause to fear. Yet I pray him to hold his hand a bit, as I find his smashers in the ribs to be, as he describes Sayers' hits, 'simply terrific ! !'

I wish to say 'under the rose,' O Spirit! that 'Morton's' *mortifying* insinuation, that I am not an adept at French, is simply scandalous—a libel upon my character—as I not only did eat, drink, and sleep in Paris, once upon a time (and a time it was) for more than a week !—Think of that !—and even passed through Brussels, where—as Sir G. F. B. ('the Baronet') says of gentlemen from the United States of America —'they pitch it in considerable smart'—but more than all that (as if anyone would require more), I most undoubtedly resided—had a *carte de residence*, which was obliged to be had at that time there—at Tahiti, subsequent to its military occupation by *Le Grand Nation*, where, you must know, the language of their conquerors is jabbered in all its native purity by barefooted and breech-clouted 'Kanakas.' And in all these localities, as in many others in various parts of the globe—which I can swear is round, having encircled it twice (would you believe it ?) in the course of ten years' ramblings—I have verified the words of another, who in speaking of the Spanish (it is applicable to all languages) says : 'The Castilian tongue may easily be acquired witnout a master ;' but as far as my individual experience goes, no study is comparable to its acquisition with a *tutoress,* who, with the charms of bright eyes, rosy lips, and clear natal enunciation, renders the task not only facile, but pleasurable. *Au revoir!* " Veritas."

In the earlier part of my story I promised my readers a description of a *marble store,* they (the readers) possibly may think had I employed an artist to sketch one, and printed the same, as a frontispiece to my book, I might have saved myself a world of trouble. Not so, reader ; no sketch or drawing would give any more idea of a marble store, than they would of a white satin dress. It requires to stand out in grand relief against a thunder cloud or a clear blue sky to be appreciated in its *exterior*, to be taken piece-meal to be understood in its *interior*.

I think I have said before that outside show is the grand object with everybody in everything, in America. Hence the object of the marble store. The old-established firm of McMoney and Goldpin are doing, as they have done for many years, a fine business. " They can put down a million of dollars, without melting an almighty ounce—*they* can! Yes, sir-r." They are content with an old-fashioned (?) built hard-upon-ten-years-ago, brick-built building, with unpretending shop front and antiquated paned windows.

The new one of Giltspoon and Gohahed (*they* have made their money somehow, somewhere) suddenly appear upon the scene, spring up like mushrooms in a night, and simultaneously with their advertisements, which run in this wise :

Messrs. GILTSPUR & GOHAHED, from Washington (*or the Diggings, or elsewhere.*—M. P.) beg to announce that they will open their NEW STORE, in BROADWAY, corner of 201st Street, with the finest Stock of JEWELLERY, ARTICLES of VIRTU, DIAMONDS, EMERALDS, PRECIOUS STONES, and *ONIONS* (*or any other nonsense.*—M. P.) in the World, on Monday, the 32nd of January (*or any other uncertain period.*—M. P.)

Come and see ! Come and see ! ! Come and see ! ! ! Come and see ! ! ! !
Come and see ! Come and see ! ! Come and see ! ! ! Come and see ! ! ! !
Come and see ! Come and see ! ! Come and see ! ! ! Come and see ! ! ! !

Up springs (mushroom-like also) a gigantic edifice, marble externally, plate-glass windows, iron sashes, and *nobby* doors.

" Guess that whips old McMoney and Goldpin's concern, anyhow !" says the crowd, and gaping, the crowd rushes to see the tempting display of the aforesaid jewellery, &c., in Messrs. G. and G's. glittering windows. And " This won't suit !" says Messrs. McMoney and Goldpin ; and thereupon, after a very short consultation with Messrs. Stone and Planner, the eminent builders, contractors, and so forth, and a cursory glance at their bank account, in six months after, up rises a similar marble giant, a story higher than that of their opponents ; and, not content with having their window panes of plate-glass, the sashes and pillars must be silver-plated.   This done, away go the crowd *from* " Messrs. Giltspoon and Gohahed" *to* the new fabric of " McMoney and Goldpin ;" whereupon, a conversation ensues between the partners of the first-named firm, and they (if not *quite* bankrupt) " right away" proceed to either stick up an additional story (if their gingerbread pile will, or they think it will, *stand* it), or put in a new and elaborate shop-front, or insure the concern, and set fire to it, or some other startling method of making the firm (shocking misnomer) of " Messrs. Giltspoon and Goahed" a *more* familiar household word than that of their opponents. And so on.

My readers will perceive, from the time I have allotted for the *getting up* of these wonderful erections—viz., six months, that real solidity is not an item in the work ; before I left New York, I had an opportunity of narrowly watching the start, progress, and finish of a marble store.   Messrs. Stump and White having made a million or so of dollars in the lower part of the city, in (*or about*) a very unpretending little shop (not so large as my frien Bright's, at Leamington), determined on investing or sinking (as the case may ultimately prove) £40,000 ! in a grand new marble store, in an improving site, *on* Broadway.   I saw it commenced in January, and all but finished by the middle of June.   It is five stories high, and composed entirely of brick and marble, iron, and glass—not a particle of wood being used.   Under the road are cellars, in which is a huge steam-engine, buried alive, as it were : by the aid of which everything is manufactured (is that a bull ?) on the premises, even to the implements used by the artificer in his work.   Every floor is devoted to a separate description of labour, and presided over by a special inspector and director.   The Americans are very proud of their marble stores, and I think justly so.

CHAPTER XIII.

WHEN the fight came off, and the result ascertained, no Englishman's bones were safe in any of the restaurants or bars for many days, and *I* had more than one friendly warning to keep no appointment, and attend to no message, unless well armed, or in company. My pen-and-ink assailants were, of course, more bitter than before, and if Mr. D., of *Bell's Life*, knew the risks I ran, and the loss I sustained, in publicly upholding his conduct against American opinion, *en masse*, he would have long since made me a present of all the back numbers of *Bell's Life*, handsomely bound, *at least*.

I found continuing the Hope Chapel Entertainments out of the question, and, as at this time I received an intimation from England that my Theatrical Account had been accepted and approved, I turned my thoughts homeward. You will see, reader, by this, and the thinning of the unread leaves of my little volume, that our task of writing and reading draweth to a close.

We kept our promise of paying Troy a visit, and were very successful, the Sayers and Heenan fever not raging there quite so hotly as in New York. Albany is a charming little town, about five miles from Troy, and here, also, we did "*good business;*" here, also, we saw something so well worth seeing, that I must ask you a question—

Have you heard or read of "The Shakers?" No! Well, I will tell you all about them. They are a very queer lot, indeed. One Sunday morning—a very fine one—having on the previous night received all necessary instruction and information, off we went in a "*neat turn-out*" (the carriages for hire are better in Albany than I ever saw elsewhere, either in England or in America) and after an agreeable drive of seven miles over a hilly road, but through a highly-cultivated country, with charming views, we found ourselves at the "Shaker Village," which in itself, as an oddity, is worth seeing, being totally unlike any village in the world—at least, in my ken—and more resembling a large farm-yard, without beasts, birds, or implements of agriculture, of any description, barring a pump. On our arrival (we were rather late), we discovered ourselves in the midst of at least a hundred vehicles of all sorts and sizes. The *company* had arrived, we were told, and were then in the place of worship, witnessing the ceremonies, or, as Lucille somewhat professionally termed it, " the performance !" A sort of harmonious howling reaching our ears at this moment, warned us that the curtain was up (I am afraid *I* said *that !*), and in we went.

Now, reader, picture for yourself a large square white-washed room, one end of it occupied by a brilliant assemblage of ladies and gentlemen, dressed to death, seated on benches sloping from the floor almost to the ceiling. This was the audience. The performers consisted of some two hundred males and females—I believe, men and women—but as unlike men and women as possible. The men had their hair cut short in front, and hanging down their backs ; white cotton neckcloths, with long ends ; coats, with tails down to their heels, and waistcoats of brown serge, with large flap pockets ; trousers of the same material—loose in the seat, and tight in the leg, reaching half way down the calf—white cotton stockings, and enormous shoes. I never saw such shoes !

The women hadn't a vestige of hair to be seen, and wore skull caps or a species of (what I believe is termed) " *penny caul* ;" white silk, or cambric handkerchiefs, pinned down fore and aft ; and skirts of the same material as the men's breeches, fitting tight over their——well, their *hips*. The nearest approach to *crinoline*, I computed at a short yard in circumference. White stockings, and shoes, closely allied in shape and size to those of the males. Each female had a white pocket-handkerchief hung over the left arm, waiter-wise, of snowy whiteness, but as stiff as buckram.

As we entered, the hymn, psalm, or symphony, was concluded, and being ushered to seats (ladies on one side, gentlemen on the other), in the dress circle, by a stout party in the same, " get up" as the others, there we sat for upwards of ten minutes, in total silence, save now-and then a slight giggle among the audience, or a loud nasal performance by some one afflicted with a cold in the joint assembly. *They were all*

employed—every mother's son and daughter of them were beating the
DEVIL'S TATTOO *with their fingers on their knees!*

"They're doing the 'daddy, mammy,' sir," whispered Stocks, who was
sitting by my side. "Wouldn't it be beautiful if our drummers in
barricks was as quiet over it?"

I gave him a kick, as at this moment some one began a speech, not
a prayer; it appeared that prayers were over. It was nearly word for
word as follows:

"Brothers and sisters, I wish to say a few words before we disperse.
Praise the Lord! I've been six years, next fall, admitted into the bosom
of the Shakers, and I can say I have never wished to depart from their
ways, and I have fattened in the Lord." ("Which is the chap as is
speaking?" said Stocks. "Well, he *is* fat, sure*ly* !") "And I have never
done no harm to any of my brothers and sisters. I may have trans-
gressed in my ways afore I com'd among my brother Shakers, but
nobody asked any questions, and nobody wanted any money." ("How
jolly!" quoth Stocks). "What we get, we share." (Hear, hear! from
Stocks, loud enough to elicit an alarming scowl from the Usher). "And
we live happy and comfortable one with the other; and those who don't
like, needn't jine us. We worship the Lord in our own way, and we
keep ourselves to ourselves. If any of my brothers or sisters wish to
address the meeting, let 'em do so. Praise the Lord! Amen."

Several brothers and sisters "followed" in the same style—one
awfully ugly female stating that ever since she had "jined the Shakers,
no one had never interfered with her," which drew from Stocks an indignant, "I'd like to know who *would.*" A little *music* followed, after
which all the men rose and deliberately *took off their coats,* and hung
them on pegs in the wall—Stocks excitedly insisting that they were
going to "*wrastle.*" They, however, proceeded to perform the queerest
lot of manœuvres I ever witnessed, singing all the time a sort of sailors'
Yo-heave-ho-and-up-she-comes chorus.

They advanced in line, in polka time, then right-about-turned, formed
into fours—(I thought I *must* have roared—Lucille *did,* for I heard
her)—stood at ease and attention, and finally formed square, and were
addressed by somebody in the centre; they then opened out into

quarter distance column, and sat down, when I'll be hanged if the women didn't, like a reserve battalion, go through the same *religious exercises*, were addressed by a female inspecting officer, and then the two armies joined forces, and danced in couples all round the room, to an *air* very like "Dixies' Land," but not quite *it*. This ended the Entertainment, when, after the audience had been partly complimented and partly condemned, for their orderly or disorderly conduct (I told Lucille afterwards, she ought to be ashamed of herself), by the before-mentioned Usher, the whole assemblage broke up.

Being Sunday, we could not see the arrangements of the Shakers' habitations, which, I was told, they are very proud of showing to visitors. The women live in separate houses to the men, and I believe there is no marrying—so I don't know how they manage to keep up the Shaker stock. Perhaps, as Stocks suggested, "They steal the young 'uns!" They had large farms, and—so much for the Shakers.

From Albany, we went to Philadelphia and Baltimore ; but as my reader must now consider my "Theatrical Trip" ended, we must be permitted to expect to be let off with a very short notice of these places—*en passant*, I may mention that they are first-rate theatrical towns. It was at Philadelphia that Jenny Lind caused such a sensation, when she appeared ten years ago at the Chestnut-street Theatre, that tickets were sold by auction, and the *first* "knock down" was 625 *dollars!*—something like £125 !

An ancestor (I believe) of a friend of mine in the Artillery, founded the state of *Penn*sylvania, of which Philadelphia ought to be the capital, but isn't—a much smaller town, called Harrisburg, some one hundred miles off, enjoying that distinction. Father Penn's ability in nomenclature must have been very limited, as he christened all the streets as if they had been trees, so we find a Vine-street, Mulberry ditto, Chestnut ditto, Walnut ditto, Pine, Cedar, and Spruce dittos ; and when used up in that line, he fell back upon Arithmetic. Thus :—*First-street*, *Second* ditto, *Third* ditto, up to any number.

Every street in Philadelphia has a railway through it. Fact!—a railway !—that is, the omnibuses, though *drawn* by horses, *run* on rails, which makes riding or driving, to those who are not *in* said "busses," not only unpleasant, but dangerous, and utterly spoils the appearance, to English eyes, of what would otherwise be wide and handsome thoroughfares.

CHAPTER XIV.

BALTIMORE.

BALTIMORE!—what shall I say of Baltimore?—merely that our stay
was so short, that we had only time to think we shouldn't like to end
our days there. At Baltimore, however, I, for the first time, had an
opportunity of seeing slaves, slave-owners, and their plantations.

What is my opinion of Slavery?

Always maintaining the opinion that no one should express an opinion
on any matter, with which he is not thoroughly acquainted, *my* opinion
on Slavedom cannot be worth having. The Yankee query-nuisance
of "What do you think of our country?" is here changed for
"What do you think of our slaves?"—and it is curious to note
the anxiety depicted in the countenance of the querist. *My* answer
was invariably to both, "I have not seen enough of it," or "them."
This reply, one evening (the first on our arrival), drew from a
tall, intelligent-looking person, whom I, by chance, had entered into
conversation with at the bar of the hotel, the following *polite* and pithy
invitation: "You are a Britisher—an Englishman, I reckon—least-
ways, you don't talk like a Frenchman. Now, just you go and take
your name off old H——'s book, and fetch away that darned handsome
gal I saw a hanging on to you, and come right slick away to my diggings—I guess we'll just fix your 'pinions about slaves pretty considerable, darned unalterable—yes, sir-r."

This *(the first invitation to any man's house I had received in America)*,
I at once accepted for myself, Lucille agreeing to stay, and do the
dutiful, with her mother. A delightful drive of ten miles brought us to
the plantation, and for the pleasant hours I spent thereat, I here tender
my thanks to my kind host, who, should he ever read this book, will, I
trust, pardon my having chronicled his little peculiarity of speech, and
only see in my narrative a grateful reminiscence.

Much as I had heard of planter hospitality, all fell far short of what
I experienced at the hands of Mr. W—— and his pretty wife. Their
house—a model of neatness, and superbly furnished—reminded me of

an East Indian bungalow, having only one story, and all the principal sitting and bed-rooms being on the ground floor. The servants—all slaves—were domiciled, with the exception of the nurse and W's. own body servant, in out-houses some fifty yards from the dwelling, and when wanted, were summoned by ringing a hand-bell. Now, I'm not going to abuse my kind host's hospitality, by giving to My *world* of readers an account of how and when we breakfasted, or off what we dined, or whether the plate *was* plate, or only plated ; whether the customs ot the house were entirely " *up to*" an Englishman's ideas of comfort, or certain peculiarities, altogether pleasing to me. Suffice it to say, that I never lodged and boarded with a happier family, or one who strove more to minister to the amusement of their lodger and boarder.

Of course, Mr. W—— and I had *arguments* on and concerning Slavery, as I suppose there's not an Englishman *out* that wouldn't have *his* say upon the subject; but I invariably, even in my own opinion, got the worst of the bout, and am bound to confess that there is no class of servants in *my* ken, who *do so little for their wages*, as slaves. They are the fattest, laziest, and " *cheekiest*" of mortals. Not one of them, un-less compelled—which compulsion the simple fact of being a slave alone accomplishes—would ever stir a finger in labour. Nature has been so bountiful to the land they live in, that its fertility offers in itself a premium to indolence.

The Northerners may *say* as they please of, but, in fact, they *do, in* the matter of Slavery, all in their power to keep it up, and that, too, in its *worst shape*, for they it is who trap the wretched creatures upon foreign shores, who fit out those floating hells, and, when escaping pepper from our cruisers, run their filthy half-carrion cargo into some slave port—thereby, if not compelling, at all events encouraging, the slave-owner to increase and multiply his slave stock, by these disgusting means. My friend W. concluding one of our *arguments*, said, " There is scarcely a slave-owner in the country but would rather be without *imported* slaves. I wouldn't give one of our own Virginny-raised Niggers for a dozen sich vermin !"

It is this importation of *blacks* that keeps up the race of *slaves*—with-out it, Slavery would abolish itself. There are thousands of slaves now in whose veins there is hardly a stain of black-blood, and the *whiter* a slave becomes, the more he knows and feels *Knowledge and feeling are direct antidotes to Slavery*. Ergo, the larger the increase of slaves, *without the aid of the hateful slave trade*, the sooner will Slavery be swept to the winds, and the slave advocate to the ocean.

There's a speech for you !

Well, we must leave Baltimore and the blackies now, and hurry homewards. I picked up Lucille (who, all the time I was away, laboured under a conviction that I should be kidnapped as a white Nigger, and sent to "pick cotton in de field"), and without halt or hindrance, returned to New York.

I have hurried my narrative here, as it scarcely can be looked upon as a portion of my legitimate " Trip," and it is moreover my intention, at some no very distant date, to re-visit the Southern States, having seen sufficient promise of a most interesting and amusing tour : and should such intention be carried out, I may possibly again rush into print, and give my readers a longer Chapter on my "opinions" of Baltimore.

CHAPTER XV.

ALTHOUGH Parodi and Piccolomini had taken wing, there were a vast number of Italian, German, and American feminine stars in the New York operatic firmament about this time, comprising such names as Cortesi, Colson, Gazzaniga, Strakosch (and her sister, Adelina Patti)— Fabri (who came with an immense flourish of trumpets from the Brazils, or somewhere), &c. The first-named is a fine actress, and, (though like all of them, worn to death in voice), would, I think, take a high position anywhere, having a consummate command of good and *bad* notes ; Patti is very young—I am told, not seventeen ; but the labour of "getting-up" in a score of operas, and singing them nightly for months at a spell, has worn herself and her voice to threads. The adulation of the Americans, who claim her for their own, though I believe she was born and bred in Europe, was immense, and I suppose even Piccolomini scarcely outdid her in newspaper puff and Platonic presents. Speaking of presents, I cannot here help mentioning a little incident.

We were one spare night listening to Patti, in *Martha*, and drawing " oderous" comparisons, of course, when my attention was drawn by Lucille to a party of young men who were intently gazing at our box, and on finding that I noticed them, made unmistakeable signs of wishing me to come to them. It was such a common occurrence at this time for *us* to be stared at, that at first I set down the present instance to nothing more than a little more than ordinary rudeness, and took no further notice until the fall of the curtain upon the second act. One of the gentlemen alluded to then stood up, and elevated a bouquet of consider- able dimensions towards Lucille, which, of course, drew the all now unoc- cupied eyes of the audience upon us, and, considerably annoyed, I beckoned the *gardener* to come to the box, which he speedily did, ac- companied by some five or six others. He introduced himself and his friends as Southerners, and we soon recognised in them an enthusiastic party that had almost nightly attended our Entertainments at the Hope Chapel. He, in a very gentlemanly manner, proffered the before-mentioned bouquet to Lucille, complimented us, and, of course, especially her, on the great pleasure they had received, et cetera, et cetera; and after receiving a half-promise from us to visit New Orleans before we left America, bowed himself and his party off.

When we had sufficiently recovered from the shock of this unexpected compliment, we examined the gift, and found it composed of rare exotic flowers, arranged with taste in a holder of gold and mosaic-work, studded with pearls and turquoises, and, what amused us more than all (how about your curiosity, reader?) carefully enveloped in silver paper, a small *d'oyley* of white satin, on which was printed the following lines :

LUCILLE, where art thou? why hush'd is thy song?
  Thou " Last Rose of Summer," what are you
About, that without you, you keep us so long?
  Why do not the managers " star" you?

Are we right in our fears, will for ever our ears
  With Parodi, " Pic," Patti, Cortesi
Be bored? when there's one, who can give them a " *stun*,"
  " *Take their track*"* from, and then beat them easy.

Let little " Pic" squeal, and Parodi loud peal
  Forth their notes, which some say are divine ;
We care not for " Fatty," and as for poor Patti
  From her you've quite taken the shine.

Then come to the South, and your own pretty mouth
  Shall ne'er ope, but with rapture we'll hear you,
We pray you come forth from this cold shallow North,
  And to sunny Orleans we will bear you.

Accept this sweet token, we bring you heart-broken,
  The gift itself's scarce worth your thank'ees,
And when it's grown older, then stick to the holder,
  As we will to you, though we're Yankees !

Were it not for the intrinsic value of the gift, I should have felt bound to have looked upon this precious *morceau* as a would-be-witty satire; as it was, however, we agreed that the compliment, though

---

* A Yankee term, signifying *Going a-head.*

coming in "such questionable shape," *was* a compliment, and, as such, my inserting the same in this history, proveth we, to this day, consider it. The flowers are long since faded and gone ; the holder stands before me as I write, under a glass shade, and the verses are *immortalised!*

We gave three nights' Entertainments at Brooklyn—a sort of over the-water suburbs of New York—and these were our farewell efforts to give amusement to, and extract dollars from, our American patrons. I was tired, in fact, of my "Trip"—the amount of unaccustomed anxiety and perpetual "something to do" attendant thereon, had sickened me *for the time* of acting, and I pined for steaks and bottled stout ; besides, my clothes were worn out, and Lucille said, "She was all to pieces !"

Dress, I may remark, is in New York a most expensive luxury. An ordinary suit of broadcloth can scarcely be got under 70 dols., fourteen pounds English ; and a mild Lady's bonnet is cheap at 20 dols. Talking of bonnets, reminds me of a little instance I must give you of lady-politeness that occurred one day *Heaven* knows whether it should be taken as a general sample or not—*I* don't. Lucille had rather a nobby little hat—an importation from *home*. Hats were then unknown *on* Broadway as a portion of a lady's apparel, and great was the consternation this same Lilliputian Golgotha created. The men seemed rather to like it, but the women said, "They wouldn't wear such a fixing atop of *their* head—*they* wouldn't !"

Well, as before said, "one day" Lucille and myself were doing a promenade (a thing we seldom *did* do) during the fashionable hour, down the fashionable side of Broadway. Suddenly I heard a small scream, and felt L's. arm withdrawn from mine, and looking round, I saw her standing by herself, looking wildly about, bare-headed, and her long hair streaming in profusion down her back ; a second look, showed me a lady gorgeously dressed, endeavouring to *shake off* the afore-mentioned "pork pie," which by some means had been hitched on to, and been whisked away, by the lady's parasol. Down it fell on to the saliva-stained pavement, and *poking it* towards Lucille with the point of her parasol, she said, "I guess *it's* yours, marm, and *it* has spiled my fringe —it has !" And, without further word, walked away.

Before I could recover my astonished wits, a *Gentleman* picked up the inoffensive, yet maltreated millinery, and carefully wiping it with his handkerchief, restored it to Lucille, saying, " I blush for *my* countrywoman's manners."

C. J. Culliford, lith.   22, Southampton S.t Strand.

This is a little sketch made at Newport a fashionable bathing place, and this is how they do it. —

"Which are the Ladies & which are the Gentlemen?" – just which ever you please.

CHAPTER XVI.

It was now the middle of June, and my arrangements were completed for returning to England, all but the vessel. What ship should we go by? By one of the Cunards—one of the same sort as that which had brought us out so calmly and comfortably, or some other? The Cunarder, of course. Good! Fate, however, ordained it otherwise. I had given a promise that I would *lend a passage* to a fellow-mortal who had gone to America to make his fortune, but hadn't, and who now was rampant to get back again; our party was hence a large and expensive one—including the dog, six in all. A careful analysis of the different rates and fares, as charged by the different companies, showed me a tempting *difference* in favour of the Liverpool, New York, and Philadelphia Line, which consists entirely of Screw steamers, and though I had a strong dislike to *screws* of all kinds, I determined on " doing the cheap" for once, and one fine morning found me in the office of the Liverpool, New York, and Philadelphia Screw Steamship Company's office, taking tickets for self and party, for our homeward voyage from New York to Liverpool.

I should have little more now to say but for an incident occurring at this very time of ticket-taking, which, though not of a very startling nature, were it narrated in a novel, pre-written in the writer's brain, I think my readers will allow to be singular enough to merit a page or or so, in this most veracious history.

I was standing on the steps of the steam-packet agent's office, on Broadway, in the act of carefully stowing away my tickets in a pocket-book, when a lady and gentlemen ascended them, and, pre-occupied with home thoughts engendered by the occupation, I stood, unconsciously, in their way. A polite " If you please," from the gentleman, made me look up, and so remarkable was the lady's start, as I bowed my apology, that *she* tripped over her dress, and I nearly stumbled down the steps. Why tripped the lady? Wherefore stumbled I?

Just four years ago—Good gracious! Well I am going to tell you a story, and novelists are always allowed to " conduct their reader" (&c.,

&c.,) to antecedents to explain the plot and pith of their story—I only claim the same allowance:—Just four years ago, having received a hasty summons home from my fishing quarters in Norway, I took steamer from S—— to London, and not being a particular good sailor, for my own comfort, and at a slight extra expense, I engaged, by letter, a cabin to myself. I did not reach S—— until the evening previously to sailing, and was somewhat surprised, on my arrival at the hotel, at learning that " a person from the ship had called several times to see me, and would be there again shortly." He came, and proved to be the purser of the steamer in which I intended sailing. He acquainted me that all the principal cabins were chock-full, and that a young gentleman had come on board and was in a great way because he couldn't have a private cabin, and refused to go in the public berths. Would I allow him to share mine, as there were two berths in it ?

This was a nuisance ; but after inquiring whether the lad couldn't be exchanged for a *lady*, or some other equally facetious remark, I learned that he was a youth of about fourteen, well-dressed, with a good portmanteau, and a patch over one eye ; and I gave a reluctant consent that the young gentleman might occupy my apartment that night and every other such, until we arrived at our destination.

I did not go on board until the following morning, and the vessel sailing half-an-hour afterwards, being unencumbered with luggage, save a parcel of fishing rods, basket, and knapsack, I did not go to my cabin until late in the afternoon, when, failing to discover my " compagnon du voyage," I thither proceeded, intending to see what he was like. I found the door locked. Upon my giving a smart rap on the panel, a very frightened, youthful voice, exclaimed, " Who's that ? What is it ?" I answered, " Be kind enough to open the door, young gentleman, that the part-proprietor of this establishment may enter." Whereupon, and during which, there was a sound of considerable shuffling of something into something, and shutting-up and locking of the same. The bolt was so softly withdrawn that I was not aware for some seconds that I was free to enter. I at length did so, and discovered——Nothing ! He, the mysterious youth, had " turned in," and the curtains of his berth were already drawn.

" Hilloa !" I said, " is anybody ill ?"

" Got a bad cold and head-ache, sir," responded a voice, totally unlike that I had first heard.

" Oh, never mind my boy," I said ; " I won't disturb you." To which the invisible youth replied, " Thank you, sir." And after arrangiug my few traps, I returned on deck, and thought no more of the matter until dinner-hour arrived, when I expected to see my double-voiced friend, but—didn't. I inquired of the steward if any dinner had been sent to No. 4, and he replied in the negative.

Having finished my own, I again went below ; this time the door was unlocked, but the curtains were as " hermetically sealed" as before. I asked, " Ain't you going to take any dinner ?" and got for a reply, in the same foggy voice, " Can't you let a fellow alone ?—don't want anything !"

After this, of course, inquiry was rude ; so, as there was a slight sea on, and I am always squeamish the first few hours (*squeamish*, mind !— not sick—oh, no !) I, after taking a few turns on deck, and inquiring " how her head was !" and remarking, with a T.P.C. hitch of my trousers, that it " looked dirty to wind'ard," tumbled below, and " turned in"— i.e., undressed myself, and got into my crib, which was not, as is mostly the case, above or below my companions, but opposite, and in such close proximity, that I might, had I been on a sufficiently friendly *footing*, have kicked the said companion at pleasure.

Generally, I sleep pretty well at sea, but this night I didn't—couldn't— Could *not* keep my eyes off the closed curtains of the opposite berth. I could see that they were *pinned* in two places—the heels of a pair of patent-leather boots peeped out from beneath ; there were also a coarse-looking cloak and broad-brimmed wike-awake hat on the top of a port-manteau, which last had evidently undergone violent usage in a fruitless endeavour to be " got under" the berth. I thought I detected a slight sneeze, and again a mild blowing of the nose, and the faintest moving of the curtain. I at last became convinced that an eye was looking at me —*an eye*—*one* eye—and in no ordinary way either. Not as an eye ought to look—bravely out through the half-opened curtain—no, sir ; but slily, surreptitiously, through an artificial slit, where no slit should have been. Slit, do I say ?—a very pin-hole ; but there *was* the eye ; I could see the glitter of the pupil, and the winking of the lashes, and

—puff! *out went the lamp.* The allotted time for the burning of the night-oil had expired, and we were in darkness.

" Well, *you* can't see now, any more than *I* can—that's a comfort," I soliloquized, and turning round, soon tumbled into an uncomfortable doze—so uncomfortable, that I cut it short by waking up, determined on transgressing the ship's rules, and lighting my reading-lamp—which, after many scratchings of damp (that word is *damp*, mind !) matches, I succeeded in doing, and was pleased to find that my neighbour was not aroused by the noise, and had gone off into a sound sleep. I read several pages of a most amusing and lively book, supposed to have been written by a " Retired Physician," and after surfeiting myself with an exciting description of the amputation of the lovely leg of a loving ("alas ! not wisely, but too well,") young lady, I found my eyes again irresistibly attracted to my neighbour's berth. There was a slight move of the curtains, and just as I was about to inquire if my light disturbed the youngster's slumber, something commenced to peep out from the farther edge of the berth, which, increasing in size and distinctness, resolved itself into a remarkably white foot, naked, and of exceeding smallness for a boy of fourteen, unless he were, indeed, a very little'un. Almost simultaneously with this apparition, there appeared at the Antipodes of this foot—a hand! It came out as though the owner was stretching himself, and approached to within half a yard of my nose, over the bridge of which I surveyed, with astonishment, a magnificent diamond and emerald ring upon the third finger. The arm, which was bare to the elbow, was a clean-made limb as you would wish to see, but did not look much like the right sort for pulling an oar, or handling a cricket-bat. A strange feeling possessed me ; and after a few moments, when the two delicate extremities were withdrawn from my gaze, I crept out of my berth—listened—and heard the steady breathing, as of one who slept soundly. Gently, yet with some difficulty, I drew the sharp-pointed instruments of millinery out of the curtains, and carefully shading the light from the eyes of the sleeper, I saw——an exceedingly nice specimen of a pretty *girl!* The before-mentioned patch had fallen, or been removed from her eye, and lay on the pillow. She was partly dressed in a pair of boy's blue serge trousers, and a striped cotton shirt; her jacket was off, but her waistcoat, though on, was

open, and it needed no second look to tell *what* lay beneath the carefully buttoned shirt-front. She had a slipper on one foot, but the other had
released itself and played truant, as I have mentioned. Her stockings—
Silk?—yes, sir—lay by her, in reach of her hand; her hair was a pretty head
of hair enough, and curly, but cut short, and parted like a boy's, and——
that's all, I think. A description of features would be improper, for
many reasons. I carefully adjusted the curtains, pins and all, got
noiselessly again into my crib, put out the light, and, with no end of
queer feelings, and 'mid an exciting crowd of pretty Pages, Dorotheas,
Rosalinds, and other breeched beauties, I slept soundly until morning.

But with morning came waking, and then came the unanswerable
question, " How the Dickens was I to perform my ablutions with a
lovely female in all probability watching the performance through an
established slit in the curtain. Perhaps she wouldn't—then, perhaps,
she would; and so, at last I said, " Hi ! young gentleman (I had nigh
said young lady), are you going to get up ?"

I was answered with a very husky " No."

" Very good, then ; *I* shall, for we never can get up together."

I certainly did hear the words, " Not exactly," and, I *thought*, a giggle
I said sharply, " What ?"

" Nothing; I'm going to sleep." A sneeze, and something like a
turn over—face to the *wall*.

So far, so good; and seeing there was no help for it, up I sat, and
having screwed three parts of my legs into the entirety of my trousers,
I slid out, and, starting at every splash as I gammoned a wash, I
managed to get into my garments and out of the cabin, resolving I
would never again invite any unknown young gentleman to share a
night's lodging with me.

I was congratulating myself on the fineness of the weather, which
made our arrival at London Bridge before nightfal a certainty, when
a sudden stopping of the engine, and a few inquiries, convinced me that
I was doomed to spend another night at sea, with the choice of the
deck for my bed, or my boy-lady's companionship in the cabin below.
The day passed, without sign of the young gentleman, until late in the
evening, when, apparently unaware that anything had happened to
impede our progress, up he came (I shall still call her " *he* ;") the

" wide-awake" on his head, the lower part of his face quite concealed in a voluminous muffler, and a large cloak completely enveloping his figure. I saw his nervous look around as he set his foot on deck, and and as he came aft, I went straight to him, and said, " How do you do? You are rather a late riser for a youngster." He immediately and evidently recognised me, and became more husky than ever as he answered, " I am not well. I thought we were almost in."

" In where ?"

" London, of course."

" You wont be in London to-night." (A great start and hat nearly off.)

" Heavens ! you don't say so ?"

" I do. We have injured our engines, and may be out two or three nights yet." (This I said to torment him, as I knew at latest we should be in early the next morning.)

Another ejaculation—huskiness nearly forgotten—"What shall we do?"

" We ! Who's we ?"

Slight confusion, and " Me, I mean, I——"

" Oh, you. *You* are all right ; you are quite welcome to my cabin all the time we are out."

" Thank you—thank you! But——I think I will go down stairs."

I was within an ace of offering him my arm, but recovering myself in time, allowed the discomfited youth to go " *down stairs*" without further question, and seeing his piteous expression, I determined on sleeping on deck, and leaving him in undisturbed possession of the cabin.

The night was fine, and having secured my greatest of coats and thickest of horse-rugs, and a supply of the *inevitable* " baccy," I selected a secluded and sheltered corner, and therein made up my impromptu couch. My next move was into the purser's cabin, where, in the company of that functionary, I contrived to pass a very comfortable hour or so until the " putting out of the lights," when a yawn from my companion, and the chance intimation that a heavy dew was falling, sent me off to seek my resting-place " beneath the blue canopy of heaven," &c. &c. *'Twas occupied !* My couch was *somebody else's*, my rug was a stranger's mattress, my coat his counterpane !

" Hulloa ! you sir; you are in my berth ! Get out !"

Starting up, the bright starlight revealed to me the frightened physog of the young gentleman! This *was* rich.

"What are you sleeping here for?" said I.

" Are these your things ?"

" Of course they are !"

" Then, I suppose you want them ?"

"Of course I do; and I want you to go' below."

" It is too hot."

"Nonsense! Better be hot there, than wet here."

"Oh, no! no !—*not again.*"

The huskiness had entirely disappeared, and that " Not again," was spoken in such heart-broken tones, that my mind was made up on the instant.

" I say you *must* go below."

" *Must*, sir!" And his eyes shone out like rival stars to those above us, and I could see the dew on his eyelashes.

" Yes, as a certain pilot is reported to have said, ' This is no place for thee.' "

" Why not, pray ? I suppose if I choose——"

" But allow me to say you musn't suppose *or* choose in the present case." Seeing him about to make an angry rejoinder, I placed my hand gently on his arm, and taking his *right* hand in mine said, " This is no boy's hand, and no boy's ring!" He trembled, but did not speak. " Nobody on board suspects what I know—namely, your sex. Silence ! Go below, sleep soundly, and rest assured I will not intrude upon you."

" Where will *you* sleep ?"

" Here, in the bed *you* have warmed for me," I said, cheerfully.

I felt the slightest pressure of her hand (*her* now—the murder was out), and rising slowly, she looked with expressive eyes (over which the *dew* by this time had obtained quite an effect) right into mine, and said, " You won't betray me, or make fun of me ?"

" My dear boy," (I feared some one might be within ear-shot) " trust me. What your reasons are for thus transmogrifying yourself I neither know nor care; tell me if you like, or leave it alone. You needn't thank me ; any *gentleman* would have behaved as I have, but you might, for all the precaution *you* took, have fallen in with *something else*, and then you would have been in an awful fix. But there—Good night !"

She, this time, did press my hand, and warmly ; and, as she disappeared in the darkness of the " lower region," I raised my voice, and said
" I shall be down as soon as I have finished my pipe. Good night !"
(This, because I saw one of the ship's mates hovering near). Little
sleep did I get that night, what with thinking over this adventure, if
such it may be called, and the dampness of my " dewy couch," my
eye-lids refused their functions altogether, and at daylight, when my
friend the purser vacated his nest, I shunted myself in " all standing,"
and there remained oblivious to the call of Time, as sounded by the
thousand and one clocks of London, until long after the vessel's sides
had made discordant music against the piles and fenders of the Irongate
Wharf, London Bridge. On turning out, I met the stewardess, who,
after a good look, asked me, " If I was the gentleman as slept on the
deck ?" I answered, " I thought I was," and she thereupon handed
me a carefully-folded note, wherein, on opening, I read :

" DEAR SIR,

"I cannot sufficiently thank you for your kindness and
consideration, and though curiosity does not seem to be a component
part of your constitution (I felt a slight twinge as I read *that*), I feel
inclined to give you an outline of the cause that made me your cabin
companion ; it is not likely we shall ever meet again, yet I would rather
you should *not* think altogether unfavourably of me. Call at the
Charing Cross Post Office to-morrow, for a letter addressed to *you*
there."

Me, there. " Egad ! she has the advantage of me *there,* anyway," I
mentally exclaimed. However, sure enough " to-morrow" I did find a
a letter addressed to *me* at the Charing Cross Post Office, and over a pint
of sherry and a sandwich, at the British Hôtel, Cockspur street, I read
it. Of course, I am not going to tell you, dear reader, *what* I read,
further than saying, it was a romantic (of course) story of a love-sick
young lady's escapade ; she having, in a moment of rage, at some real
or imaginary infidelity on the part of her lover (who had been travelling with herself, her brother, and her parents, through Norway) dis-
missed the faithless swain ; and he, having sworn to return home and
" 'list for a soger," or some other tomfoolery, she, repenting of her
hastiness, boned a suit of her small brother's clothes, and followed ; and
—that's all. I never saw her again   *   *   *   *

'until, as before recorded, " *the lady tripped over her dress, and I nearly stumbled down the steps.*" Why, this very lady was the very young lady *as was* the very young gentleman that lodged and *boarded* with me on the occasion I have just narrated.

Recovering herself, the pair passed on, and entered the office, but in a very few minutes returned, and this time the lady's head and veil were so much *down*, that I could not catch the expression of her countenance, but I did that of the following five words, most distinctly : " Here in half-an-hour ;" and half-an-hour, therefore, did see me there, and half a minute after my arrival, there I saw my mysterious acquaintance, who put out her hand as soon as I joined her, warmly shook mine, and immediately came to business, thus :

" You are surprised to see me, I guess ?"

" Well, I guess I am.   But how long have you taken to *guessing ?*"

" Oh, I am a regular Yankee now.   Did you see that gentleman ? That's my husband.   He's a Yankee, but a very good, fellow !   Would you know him again, if you were to see him ?"

" Certainly."

" Well, mind !   Don't you ever mention a word about our bit of fun, if you should come to know him ; because, although I have told him, and he knows all about it, I guess he don't care to hear anything more of it.   Besides, I told him I was nearly sure you were drowned in the " Pomona ;" and I am very glad you were not.   But you were nearly wern't you ?   And what are you doing here ?"

" Here ?—where ?   On these steps, or in New York ?"

" New York, of course !   Why—Oh my ! I forgot.   You ain't Captain What-do-ye-call-it ?   You are Captain Morton Price !   Changed your name, of course ; somebody wrote out, and told me all about it ! Where are you going to ?"

" To England."

" Not in the ' City of Washington !' "

" Yea, verily."

" Then you *will* meet my husband.   Well, I never !   I think I had better tell you all about it."

" With all my heart, if you won't be long about it.   But I must be ungallant enough to say that I have but a few moments to spare."

My old young acquaintance then, with marvellous rapidity, told me——
a great deal more than I may tell you, my reader. Suffice it to say,
that she did *not* marry her " bowld sojer boy," after all the disagreeables
she endured in the pursuit of him ; and her brother, whose blue serge
suit once so well fitted her, having gone on some mercantile business
to South America, she accompanied him, and married a Yankee, which
same Yankee narrowly escaped coming to England in the same ship
as his handsome wife's quondam queer acquaintance ; but I had actually
secured the last vacant berths. I made his acquaintance, nevertheless,
by chance, the very evening before we sailed, and a better informed, or
more gentlemanly American, I have not yet met, though little he
" guessed" *who* the gentleman was who played a "considerable tall
game at billiards for a Britisher" on that occasion.

CHAPTER XVII.

DEAR READER, this is the last Chapter of my first Book, and ere now your fiat hath gone forth whether it should be my *last* Book or not. I started (and I told you so) careless of criticism, and with the sole purpose of amusing myself. I, now, begin to have a feeling of regret that I have not more studied the amusement of others, than my own pastime. Why? Well, everyone has a right to seek for information, so I will answer— Because, as I glance over these pages, I feel convinced that I *could* have made so much more ("The saints forbid!" you say—Well I forgive you), so much more, of all I heard, and saw, in the land I am about to quit, than *I have done,* and regret that those whom I *do* wish to amuse and please, *may,* when they come to "FINIS" (if they ever do), smilelessly chuck the book upon the table, or whatever is nearest them, and say, " I thought he would have done better."

    *   *   *   *   *   *   *

I had not *many* friends in New York I cared about saying "Good- bye" to. There were *some,* however, and until the time came for speaking the word (the absence of which from our vocabulary would have played the deuce with ballad-writers and sentimental "walking gentlemen") *Farewell,* I did not imagine the amount of regret I should feel—yes, real, unfeigned regret. There were those Yankees, who had discovered almost against their wishes that I was "*not* so 'tarnation proud, after all!" Those "Knickerbockers," who loved to tell, when they found I cared to listen to, their tales of "How their Dutch forefathers came over in the year ONE, afore any of them darned Britishers got shovin' their noses where they didn't have no manner of ought," and "egg nogg"* ed me into a semi-belief that I agreed with them. " exiled sons of Erin," for ever hunting up their " *last quarter*" to stand drinks for the crowd, as *far as it would go* (Eh! Thomas F?); and, lastly, those Englishmen, few, indeed, who loving the land of their birth, welcomed and *warned* the new-comer. To many of these, I felt

---

* A drink must be drank (not *drunk*) to be understood.—M.P.

an indescribable—not loving—more than liking (I know the French word, but don't know how to spell it)—sort of clinging, sad-to-part-with-feeling, that no one—at least, I don't know anyone that can put on to paper! I can imagine the feelings of one who has been a long time in prison—the buoyancy of his brain, the elasticity of his step, the joyousness of his voice, his fresh brushed and combed and clean-washed toilet, on the morning of his walking out, a free man, from his confinement; and I can imagine each, pained and slackened, and dulled, and uncared for, as he meets some prison-made acquaintance, whom he knows to be, and respects as one, worthy as himself, yet, alas! not quite so lucky, and shakes him by the hand for the last time.

If my reader can imagine what I mean, he can imagine my feelings at parting with my only friends at New York. I know it *must* be a stretch of imagination, but please do it for *my* sake. From beginning to end of this little story, I have told you that I could never describe anything, so you can scarcely expect it under the present circumstances.

Well, to one and all, on Friday night, the twenty-ninth of June, I bade a kind Farewell! and the following morning found self and party on board the Liverpool, New York, and Philadelphia screw steam-ship, " City of Washington," wherein, and on, I closed my note-book, from which these pages are compiled on Thursday, the twelfth of July—on the evening of which day we were safely deposited, and taken in and done for, at the " George Hotel," Dale-street, Liverpool—and——That's all!

FINIS.